LAMBERT'S
BIRDS
of Garden and Woodland

Paintings by TERENCE LAMBERT

Text by ALAN MITCHELL

CHARLES SCRIBNER'S SONS
NEW YORK

1 3 5 7 9 11 13 15 17 19 I/C 20 18 16 14 12 10 8 6 4 2

Filmset by Jolly & Barber Ltd, Rugby
Reproduction by Adroit Photo Litho Ltd, Birmingham
Printed and bound by Encuadernaciones Belgas, S.L., Bilbao, Spain

Library of Congress Catalog Number 76-21893
ISBN 0 684 14795 5

Contents

Introduction 5

Herons 18
Sparrowhawk 20
Common Buzzard 23
Kestrel 25
Woodcock 26
Stove Dove 29
Wood Pigeon 30
Collared Dove 32
Turtle Dove 35
Cuckoo and Dunnock 36
Little Owl 39
Tawny Owl 40
Green Woodpecker 43
Great Spotted Woodpecker 44
Lesser Spotted Woodpecker 46
Wryneck 48
Pied Wagtail 50
Waxwing 52

Introduction

The distinction between birdwatchers and those who are 'interested in birds' is that birdwatchers make deliberate excursions just to see birds; others may see birds but are there for other reasons. At home both will probably attract birds to their garden and will watch these; the birdwatcher alone is likely to make lists and notes (and an ornithologist might make a study of habits), the others just watch.

Birdwatching in the more active sense is one of the best of all hobbies. It can take you to beautiful country, the fascinating wildnesses of saltings and estuaries, to unexpected oases of life in gravel-pits or old quarries, beside old canals and to odd corners of the land which one would never otherwise see. It is a healthy, open-air activity with peaks in spring, summer, autumn and winter. There is a good literature for winter evenings, but there can be few less expensive hobbies as the basic equipment is but binoculars, boots and books. It is open-ended in that there is always more to learn and it can be taken just as far as is wanted. There is a good chance of severe addiction and even at a less intense level there is enough in it to add a lease of life to those who retire from a demanding career and who, without some good compensating interest in life, cannot expect to live long.

The best starting point is the bird-table or the garden, where some birds will be familiar and can easily be identified. As is elaborated at some length below, garden birds are a selection of woodland birds which have adapted to the special environments of gardens. Gardens vary much in contents, layout, size and location and some may be used by the majority of our woodland birds. It is thus logical to combine a book on garden birds with those more particularly of woodlands, for most of the birds are the same and it would be impossible to make a good division.

Birds of Woodlands

The land birds of Britain are largely those species which inhabit woodland edges and clearings. When the ice finally retreated and before man made significant changes most of the land was covered by woodland. The only areas then of open habitat which would resemble fields were sand-dunes and their inland margins. The Skylarks, Grey Partridge, Stonechat and Wheatear will have been scarce birds confined to these areas of low coastline. Elsewhere the open land will have been that which was either too high and exposed for tree-cover or too low and wet. The high land, found only in the west and north was then, as now, an area of stunted and scattered birch or pine with heather as ground-cover and the home of Meadow Pipit, Red Grouse, Ptarmigan and, amongst the low trees, Black Grouse. The low-lying land was marsh – generally a temporary state gradually invaded by sallows, willows and alders and reverting to woodland, but with new areas being made by occasional floods and changes in the courses of rivers. The marshes held Reed Bunting, Sedge, Reed and Marsh Warbler, Water Rail, Moorhen, Snipe and several species of duck. None of the birds mentioned so far is a bird of normal gardens.

The woodland covering much of the lowlands will have been of two kinds, oakwood and beechwood. This is because woodlands in stable conditions develop inexorably and irreversibly. The first trees to colonise open land, arriving by means of airborne seed shed in great quantities (birch, sallow, willows, poplars) are adapted for growth in the full light and exposure of these open places. They themselves, however, change these conditions by giving shelter and casting shade. These same species can now no longer grow there. They can spread at the margins but seedlings within the woods fail for want of light and from competition. By now, though, the land is woodland of an open kind and attracts woodland mammals and birds which can bring in by various means the heavier seeds of other trees. Some of these are quite able to grow in partial shade and many positively need it. No tree, however, can grow as a healthy seedling under the shade of its own species. There is therefore a succession of mixtures of species, each generation able to grow in more shade than the one before, until the stage when the most shade-bearing of all suitable to the site arrives. Shade-bearing trees succeed by spreading their foliage so widely and densely that they intercept a high proportion of whatever light filters through to them. It follows that beneath these trees there is very little light indeed. Soon therefore the species adapted to the least light and which can grow on that soil is the only one able to succeed. The woodland has reached its climax. All woodlands which are undisturbed will become climax woodland in something like 500 years.

In swampy fens and by flooding rivers, the climax is alder, a habitat in winter for Redpolls and Siskins but a breeding place more used by Willow Tit and woodpeckers. Alder carrs and alder-lined rivers will have occurred widely scattered through the lowlands and the birds found in them are, in many places, garden birds. Elsewhere however, the climax woods were oak or beech. The beech is a tree with a powerful root-system able to penetrate far in search of water if the top soil is dry. That is the main reason for its ability to make impressive woods on the apparently dry tops of chalk downs where other trees cannot. It is rooting deeply into the chalk rock which always carries water. Beech roots, however, are absolutely deterred by wet surface soils or by layers of heavy wet soil. Big trees may often be seen which have blown down and which have wide-spreading but very shallow root systems and the hole they reveal has either a water-logged bottom layer or holds water, showing why the roots were only shallow. Beech seedlings can grow beneath oak trees but oak seedlings cannot grow beneath beech. Hence beech will replace oak and become the climax woodland where the soil is light, deeply drained, sandy or thin over chalk.

Beech climax wood is often fairly uniform high forest with most trees 30m tall and some often over 35m and in these places no other beech can grow, only a few evergreen native trees of holly and yew. Beech rarely live for more than two hundred years, and dead trees here and there let in sufficient light for patches of young trees and shrubs to arise in circular areas perhaps 30m across. Within these circles the same selection and succession go on until a few beech dominate the rest and rise to remake the high forest. These climax woods are habitat for Chaffinch, Nuthatch, Coal Tit, Great Spotted

Woodpecker, Wood Pigeon, Stock Dove and Woodcock in the high forest, and Wood Warbler, Blackbird, Robin and Wren in the openings.

Where the soil is too heavy or damp for beech, the oak will make climax woods. There are two native oaks, the common, English or pedunculate and the sessile or durmast oaks. The sessile oak was the first to arrive after the Ice Age and is the main species of the mountains of the west and north while the common oak dominates in the south and east. Their climax woods differ in important aspects due as much to the different densities of foliage as to the different geographical areas in which they occur. The handsome leaves of the sessile oak are evenly spread and allow the growth of few shrubs but a better herb layer beneath than the bunched, almost stalkless leaves of the common oak. Sessile oakwoods on Welsh and Scottish hillsides are the best habitat for Pied Flycatcher, Wood Warbler and Redstart.

The common oak frequently short-circuits the expected succession of species and comes in among the first pioneer trees and shrubs and thus begins to dominate at an early stage and grow straight into the climax woodland. This happens when there is a ground cover of long grasses and is entirely due to Jays. These birds assiduously collect acorns in October and ferry them considerable distances to bury them as a general enrichment of the food-holding capacity of their territories in hard weather. They like to bury them by or beneath a tussock of grass, but they retrieve only a small proportion and the remainder sprout and grow.

It is now thought that oak climax wood, which covered so much of lowland Britain was seldom like the oak high forest known today in woods which were planted or have a history of management. It was more open and may usually have had grassy clearings where the many minor species of native tree will have grown. There will have been areas of light soils where the oak would not predominate but the beech will have been unable to reach. Depending on the soil, various associations of other trees, shrubs and herbs will have flourished in scattered areas.

Pure oakwoods are not a rich habitat for birds. Thickets of young oak attract few species and those only when passing through. Large blocks of high oak forest in summer seem to hold nothing but endless Wood Pigeons and Chaffinches, although there are usually Great, Blue, Coal and often Marsh Tits, Tree-creepers, Nuthatches, Great Spotted and perhaps Lesser Spotted Woodpeckers, and in those parts with most bramble, Blackcaps, and if there is whortleberry in the ditches, Wood Warblers. In the winter the great feature is the roving bands of tits with Goldcrests, Tree-creepers and Lesser Spotted Woodpeckers, also sometimes there will be Woodcock.

The richest part of oak or any other woods, for birds and usually plants too, is the edge. This is true generally of any habitat and the 'edge effect' is a byword for diversity in ecology. Being an edge implies a change from one habitat to another. In Nature these edges are very rarely abrupt (a cliff edge is one that is). One habitat merges into the next and there is a zone which is neither habitat but has features of both, and these give it its own distinction as a third habitat. It will be richer in species of all sorts than the habitat each side because it shares some species with each and has some of its own as well. This zone of change has been given its own name. It forms an 'ecotone'. The ecotone between lake and meadow is marsh, between estuary mud and hinterland is salting, and between woods and meadow it is scrub. All these are rich in plant varieties and in animals and hence are favoured areas for watching birds.

The sort of climax oak woodland described above has a considerable proportion of ecotone between woodland grassy glade and between pure oak and mixed woods. It was thus far more varied in birdlife than is pure oakwood and a large number of the birds then abundant were birds of the ecotone of woodlands to grass. This means that they are birds which will take to the sort of garden that has been the great distinction in British horticulture and the pride of the British countryside, the large landscaped estates with woodland garden, relatively undisturbed and shrubberies with lawns, arboreta, and copses for game-birds.

Birds in Gardens

The kinds of bird seen in any garden depend rather more on the general surroundings of the garden than on what is in it. Few gardens are large enough to make their own habitats and a high proportion depend entirely on birds which breed elsewhere. A city garden smaller than a city square might house breeding Starlings, House Sparrows and possibly Blackbird, but it will depend upon the nearest churchyard with Lawson cypress for any Greenfinches and on the nearest park for Blue Tits and any other birds. A garden on the edge of a forest need have nothing but a puddle and mown grass and a post for perching in order to have thirty or more species within its confines. In very open areas a single bush will be used continually by a variety of birds.

The conventional suburban garden, a strip of lawn bordered each side by flower-beds or shrubs and with vegetables at the bottom is not a unit to any bird. The whole of the area between the rows of houses should be seen as a single habitat, ignoring the fences. Birds use the fences as song-posts and any that breed will nest in the bushes which are usually next to the fence, so the territories will centre on the fences and range each side of them. It is evident how the local Starlings keep an eye on the kitchen scraps put out anywhere within the area as a whole and descend in a brawling mass where the newest pickings are. The Heron likewise surveys for goldfish at dawn.

Such areas of suburban gardens are habitats of a great variety of plants with some bushes, usually some fruit and other trees (although too often these are only sycamores which are of minimal interest to birds), and mown grass. They fall short of the forest glade in lacking woods each side, uncut grass growing into the bases of the bushes, probably in the diversity of insects, often cover, and always, in one way or another, freedom from disturbance. A number of the woodland-edge birds have adapted themselves to these conditions and these gardens will have breeding populations of Jackdaws, Starlings, House Sparrows, Great and Blue Tits, Dunnock, Song Thrush, Blackbird and Robin and sometimes Goldfinch, Greenfinch, Mistle Thrush and Wood Pigeon. The benefits they find here which are lacking in the woods are abundant food, especially in winter, and warm roosts in evergreen shrubs and trees not found in the woods and around houses and sheds. These are the town garden birds.

In this sort of area quite an improvement can be made by a single owner if he can withstand uninformed criticism and break completely away from the idea that a garden must be artificially trim, weedless, clipped, pruned, sprayed, and constantly worked in. Some lawn area should be mown as this benefits Blackbirds, Thrushes and Starlings, but some should be left except for an annual autumn cut to keep it as grass and wild flowers. The main thing is cover, mixed evergreen and deciduous, beside the grass, some posts or small trees for perches and a small, shallow pool. No spring tidy-up can be allowed as birds always breed before we think they do and all that pruning and clipping disturbs and uncovers nests. Such a garden will be both a refuge and a breeding-place and the more of a contrast it is with the neighbouring gardens the more full of bird-life it will be. The open area of grass is essential and will attract far more birds than if the whole plot were to be scrub.

It is however unlikely that a bird-orientated garden of that sort would increase the *diversity* of species within that group of gardens. Even large town parks, which are mainly playing-fields, flower-beds and clipped shrubbery but which usually include one small area of sheds, leaf-pit or bonfire site, out of bounds where a pair of wrens may breed, have otherwise the same restricted number of species as the gardens, because they are very similar terrain. The park, however, having large areas of uniform field may attract in winter small flocks of Fieldfare and Redwing if there are some tall trees around the margins of the field, where the garden complex is quite unsuitable for these thrushes and will see no more than occasional half-starved wanderers in severe weather. In the autumn, any small patch of cover may be used by one or two of the myriad small migrants which pass over even city areas. The bird-garden in the suburbs, like the shrubbery by the concrete-sided lake in the city park may have a Chiffchaff or Willow Warbler using the cover as a centre from which to make sallies after insects, feeding to regain strength before moving on. It is the cover which it most needs; the insects are widespread but the bird must retreat to cover between flights to catch insects.

Larger and Rural Gardens

On the outskirts of country towns and in outer semi-suburban areas and in villages, gardens are less regular in shape, not crowded together and often bordered by remaining fragments of woods or by fields or commons. This increases the number of species in these gardens greatly because to the birds such gardens are a part of the woods or fields but with a greater diversity of habitat. These gardens in fact will be used by, or at least see or hear frequently, every species which is in the surroundings. Where there is birch in the woods or on the commons, Great Spotted Woodpeckers will come into gardens for scraps and nuts; Green Woodpeckers will search the lawns for the yellow ant, Redpolls will come to seeding birch and sorrel and Siskins for the nut-bags as well. Jays will keep an eye on the peas and on nests of small birds and Magpies have their equally beady eye on the kitchen scraps. Gorse or blackthorn in the area will ensure bands of Long-tailed Tits roving through in winter and a pair on the bird-table at a regular hour during the spring.

This kind of garden, an extension of the countryside, can be of the utmost value in preserving woodland-edge fauna and flora where the built-up area is spreading. Each garden containing bushes and areas not intensively used or cultivated can, unless too isolated, be an oasis for many birds, like Blackcap, Chiffchaff and Turtle Dove, and is part of a corridor linking with other similar gardens and spare plots to keep alive the genuine countryside birds amidst what will otherwise be doomed to be just the limited town-garden bird population, of which there is already sufficient. It is in this situation that the carving up of larger gardens into building-plots and infilling does so much lasting damage. However many trees are saved by preservation orders, the destruction is the same, for it cannot be emphasised sufficiently that single trees with paving mown grass or other used land beneath them are of no use to any but a few town birds for breeding and their preservation does nothing for the more interesting countryside birds. The old, gnarled, moss and lichen-covered apple trees and the haw-thorn scrub which are the source of the desirable species are never given such protection. Unfortunately the owners of large gardens are bound to be tempted by the money, and justification is at hand in the ridiculous idea that the garden is too big for them because, unable as they are to cut, mow, trim, dig, weed and tidy up, nature is taking over. This is an unthinkable horror and a disgrace among the neighbours – a patch of land escaping, untamed, dereliction looming, wildlife reasserting itself to threaten the lobelia, gravel paths and dogs; a source of countless weeds and nameless monsters. That this could be the ideal background to a well-kept garden is rarely considered.

An intensively kept ornamental garden is a delightful sight and is to be encouraged and welcomed. On its own, it is however a land-use of very limited appeal to birds. Weedless soil and closely mown grass offer no breeding site at all but give good feeding to Pied Wagtails, Starlings, and the thrushes including Blackbird and Robin. Herbaceous borders give low cover in summer and some insect food if they are not too assiduously sprayed (perhaps also if they are sprayed too much, for predatory insects are killed too, and resistance among the others is a possibility), but no breeding sites. The shrubs, pruned or unpruned, will encourage the breeding of Song Thrushes, Blackbirds and Dunnocks, but their cover and insect life will provide for a large number of birds. If these are all the garden comprises, though, it will rely for all but the few town-garden birds which can breed (and perhaps the Pied Wagtail, which should breed in the thatch or in a shed roof) on other less intensively cultivated gardens or the open countryside for its birds.

If the garden is of sufficient size to be providing another site for a house, it should be possible for the intensive ornamental garden to be near the house that is there and for this to tail off towards the part which makes it 'too big to manage' in grassy glades or bays with ornamental shrubs giving way to unmown grass growing up into wild shrubs and trees. Wild flowers can be encouraged in many ways and will bring butterflies, and the wild area gives a background to the highly ornamental part. It also gives breeding places for the many species of countryside birds which would like to frequent the intensive area but can do so only if they breed nearby. A garden full of birds is a real, living garden whereas one without birds or insects arouses the feeling that it could be better done in plastic.

Birds and Exotic Trees

The great variety of plants grown in gardens is an advantage to birds despite the fact that nearly all the species are exotic. Birds show no interest in where a plant comes from or the fact that their species can never have encountered them before. If the plant gives cover, food or breeding or roosting sites they will use it happily. Examples are legion but a few show this remarkably well. The Lawson cypress is one of a group of cypresses which are found only in North America, China and Japan. No species of bird native to Britain can have met any of these in the wild. The Lawson cypress was unknown before 1854 when it was found near the California-Oregon boundary and was introduced to a nursery in Edinburgh. Until 1860 there were very few plants and it can only have been common and of large size after 1900. Today it is in every town park, churchyard and large garden, in every village and many suburban gardens. Everywhere this tree is a centre of bird activity. The town Greenfinches and Goldfinches breed in it, Siskins eat the seeds, Song Thrushes and Blackbirds breed in it and sing from its top, where they compete with Collared Doves, Blue and Coal Tits use it for cover, and Goldcrests almost infest it. It gives the high cover the birds want where it is in short supply.

Some exotics have little interest to birds, as for example the sycamore, but some of the few native trees are of no great attraction either, like the holly. It is noticeable how some exotics are chosen for nesting sites in preference to native species where they are both available. A good example is a wood of larch in an area of oak and birch. There will be more Redpolls, Bullfinches, Goldcrests and birds of prey in the larch than elsewhere. For another example the Douglas fir is quite alien to Europe and equally attractive to Goldcrests and birds of prey.

Some people regard all conifers as inimical to birdlife. This is patently untrue. Our native flora is sadly lacking in evergreen high cover. The winter wind howls through the deserted oakwoods and beechwoods. The presence of a clump or strip of spruce or Lawson cypress planted for game-birds transforms this and becomes the centre of birdlife.

Listening to Birds

In the accounts which follow, of each bird pictured, there is a noticeable and deliberate emphasis on their calls and songs which leads to a rash of faintly ludicrous non-words in quotes. These should be read aloud, if only in the mind, to achieve their effect. Most readers would probably be bashful about emitting sudden cries of *'tissick, tissick, grrrk-grrrk!'* or even a modest *'pink-pink'* in a full compartment in a train or in a reading-room, but these phrases can be imagined as said with some verve, without causing raised eyebrows all round. They are important because identification is the first and vital step towards knowing more about the bird you are watching and without it birdwatching is nothing more than a vague aesthetic experience.

The natural first move in identifying a bird is to see it and to consult pictures in a bird guide. The books are necessary but they should also be used for identifying the source of unknown calls and songs as soon as possible. For knowing a bird by its sounds is far and away the most reliable, elegant and powerful method of identification, useful at all times. There are many reasons for this, some connected with the different properties of light and sound and some with the human mind. Light travels in straight lines – you cannot see a bird behind a haystack nor in a deep thicket. The eye needs a certain level of light to see at all – you cannot see a bird in the dark, and you cannot see colours at all by moonlight or at dusk or dawn. You cannot see in a fog; you cannot see behind you, and when looking intently in one direction you will notice only movement in anything outside a very narrow field; a static object there is not really seen. The light reflected from a bird varies in colour with the quality of the incident light. In the rising or setting sun, colours have a pink cast, especially all whites. A few plumages or parts of them are iridescent and refract light. These change even more with conditions; a kingfisher may look deep blue at times, pale green at others.

Worse is to come. The eye is an imperfect observer, easily misled, not a camera. The information goes first to the optic ganglia then to the brain and is processed extensively before it becomes what we think we see. A vast amount of interpretation is done in the light of our past experience, clues are used to impart perspective for example, and a big exaggeration of size at a distance is built in. Patterns are altered, some details exaggerated, some neglected, some invented, but the result, a strange contorted personal view, comes to the brain – so we insist it is inherently exact. It is an exact account of what our brains have made of it but need have little relationship to what our eyes saw. Every naturalist has to try to persuade inquirers that the red on a Great Spotted Woodpecker's head is but a patch on the nape; that the Wryneck so well described but so much too big and on the lawn in December is a Mistle-thrush. Worse still, so many problem birds are seen suddenly, in a flash and gone, and when events happen in an un-coordinated rush, they tend to be interpreted in random or reverse order and usually quite falsely. Even experienced observers are not immune. Two flushed a bird at dusk from the edge of a pond. One saw a Snipe, the other a Heron. Had it called, there could have been no errors or doubts. To be reliable, visual records need to be made in good light with steady observation.

Sound is a contrast with light in all these features. It travels round obstructions – a bird can be heard from behind a haystack, in a deep thicket or marsh and through a fog. And unlike the eye, the ear is a true recorder: no unconscious interpretation or distortion occurs. Again, in a sudden rush of different sounds, the practised ear detects and records the various calls in an astonishing way which is not understood. This well known 'cocktail-party effect' is baffling because the medley of sound arrives at the brain from the cochlea of the ear as a single complex wave-form like the track on a gramophone record, and yet the components of the single voice to which we are listening are somehow extracted. When a mixed flock is disturbed un-expectedly and flies off, the birdwatcher can unhesitatingly reel off the species heard, Chaffinch, Linnet, Yellow-hammer, Greenfinch, Red-poll . . . when the eye may see but a flutter of chaffinches. If there is a single Spotted Redshank in a departing flock of two thousand Com-mon Redshanks, it is unlikely to be seen but it will be outstandingly obvious to the ear, as will one Willow Tit among three hundred other small birds in a woodland flock.

Even that is not all. Many species closely related look similar and some may need close visual observation to be separable. Birds use calls as contacts, challenges or alarms, and songs to attract mates and repel rivals. Other species can manage their own affairs but each must communicate with its own members. And the more they resemble each other in plumage the more important it is that the calls and songs be unmistakably different. Hence birds do all the identification work for us when they utter a sound. Marsh and Willow Tits, Willow Warbler and Chiffchaff, Carrion Crow and Rook, all are instantly separable by their sounds. Further again, the poorer the light the more they need to use contact calls; in fog or when flying at night. With very few exceptions, sound clues, unlike sightings, are unambiguous, you can either hear a bird and hence know what it is or you cannot hear it at all. The only necessity is to learn what birds say.

Learning bird calls is only a matter of following up every unknown sound to identify the bird making it. With a good view of the bird uttering, the two memories are filed away so that on next hearing the call, the brain provides a picture of the bird. Every human brain has an unused capacity greater than that used; it does it good to exercise it a little. It must be emphasised that the un-musical are as adept at this as the musical and some of the best birdwatchers at identifying bird sounds are quite tone-deaf.

A useful hint is to learn the voice rather than what the bird says. That is, some birds will give many versions of their calls but the voice in which they are made is the same. For example, the Great Tit has numerous calls and variants of its song which would be very hard to learn individually, but they come unmistakably from a Great and not a Coal Tit because their voices differ. Poor mimicry is in this way not deceiving; the Robin is still a Robin not a Blackcap or Willow Warbler however much it tries to be.

A great merit of the acceptance of sound for personal records is that birds can be recorded in marshes, thickets and woods just by walking round or past them especially in the early breeding season, without the disturbance and destruction caused by having to wade or struggle in to flush the bird in these fragile habitats, which need all the protection and peace they can have.

GREY HERON
Ardea cinerea

The Heron does not look like a bird of either woodlands or gardens but is one nonetheless of both; and unexpectedly for such a large vulnerably slow bird, it survives well near towns and in London. The nests, which become huge over the years, are generally in trees – often oak, but Scots pines or crack willows are also used, and where trees are few heronries may be found in bushes or on the ground. The birds, which are dispersed widely over the countryside in winter, begin to assemble in the heronry area in early spring, and the male takes possession of a nest or potential nest-site, advertising his presence and displaying at nearby females by stretching the head and neck right up, while making a gurgling sound. Then he droops the neck over his back, still with the bill pointing up, and slowly lowers his body on the nest or branch. The chicks feed on food regurgitated by their parents by plunging their bills in the old birds' crops. There may be little suitable water for feeding within two miles or more, but at dawn the heron will visit any ditch or pool. Many a suburban gardener knows that his goldfish are part of a heron's breakfast, although he may not be up in time to see the bird at dawn surveying the situation and looking absurdly incongruous on a tree-top in a suburban road. Their favourite food is eels and this involves having a lot of slime on the plumage. Herons have powder and a comb for this, a tract of feathers being rudimentary and breaking down into powder, the 'powder-down'; and the comb is on the middle toe. In flight the huge, broad black and grey wings flap ponderously, the heavy head is brought back nearly to the wings for balance and the legs trail behind with a toe often projecting upwards visibly. When disturbed the Heron makes a resounding *'frarnk!'*. In the winter many are seen along the shoreline especially by western Scottish sea-lochs.

18

SPARROWHAWK
Accipiter nisus

Hawks have short, broad wings and long broad tails. These give them the manoeuvrability in their dashing hunting-flight through woods, sweeping low along rides and hedges and suddenly darting round or over the bushes. Falcons have long, narrow wings for fast pursuit in the open. In normal flight the sparrowhawk is much too like a Wood Pigeon in shape and size, but it alternately flaps and glides for several seconds, and shows a prominent white patch under the tail. On a fine spring morning a pair or two will often sail and soar to great heights with their short, broad wings fully spread and outer feathers separated making a jagged edge to the wing. A garden where birds are well fed on the outskirts of a town may attract a sparrowhawk, which also comes for a daily meal – one of the other birds. The female is much the bigger of the pair and has prominent white eyebrows and yellow legs, while the male is dark blue-grey above and orange-brown beneath. They are silent birds except when near the nest, and occasionally when sailing, when a persistent '*kek-kek-kek*' is uttered. The nest is a large platform of sticks about eight to twenty metres up in a tree, preferably of larch or other conifer, and often built up from the old nest of another species. Four or five nearly spherical brown-blotched eggs are laid.

BUZZARD
Buteo buteo

The Buzzard is a bird of the western wooded hills. A line drawn from Southampton to Elgin would have Buzzards on its western side wherever there are hills with trees, but scarcely any on its eastern side. They have been unable to spread eastward largely because of illegal shooting. In parts of Devon, notably eastern Dartmoor, and in mid-Wales and by the coastal flats of Argyll, one expects to see two or three in the air and one on a telegraph-pole every half-mile. In flight Buzzards either labour along with majestic deep flaps or sail at several hundred feet on spread, broad wings with the tail fanned, sweeping round in rather small circles. When perched on a roadside pole they allow quite a close approach before lifting away with a strong flap of the wings, and seem to remember only at the last moment to take their big yellow legs too. The call rings out over the woods with a sharp beginning and a fading end, like '*pee-you*', which is probably the origin of the name 'Buteo'. Sometimes Buzzards will ride the strong up-draught from a hill across a wind and at times they may have to reduce the lift from their big wings by partially folding and raising them to prevent being carried away upwards. The bulky nest, in a tall tree or sometimes on the ground, will hold three eggs, blotched and streaked brown.

Rabbits were their main diet until the spread of myxomatosis after 1954, which caused nearly total failure for a year or two in the Buzzard's breeding. Numbers have now stabilised, a little lower in some areas, with the birds eating small mammals, lizards, worms and beetles.

23

KESTREL
Falco tinnunculus

The Kestrel is a small falcon and is easily the most numerous bird of prey. It had been attracted to wide arterial roads forty years ago and is now a feature of the motorway verges and embankments. Here, as on marshes and open heaths, it can detect the movements of big insects and of rodents despite the lack of high perching places that other birds of prey need, by hovering. It heads into the wind and keeps stationary with great precision by flying at exactly the speed of the wind. In a strong wind this is no great problem, but a light wind makes adjustments necessary for supporting the bird at such a slow ground-speed: it holds its wings more forwards, which tips the bird up so that it is flying partly upwards and its body and spread tail catch more of the wind both to lift the bird and to hold it back.

The Kestrel is often seen in cities, where it may breed in church or other towers, and around ruins and cliffs, which are favourite nesting places. It is common on farmlands everywhere, except in East Anglia, and hunts over sand-dunes and saltings. It is fond of sitting on telegraph wires and posts and the male makes an attractive picture as he flies off showing a copper-brown back and bluish head and tail, the latter tipped white and black. It is a silent bird except around the nest, when it frequently utters a panicky, quavering, shrill 'kee-kee-kee . . .' The usual diet is small mammals with small birds taken from the ground in winter, but in summer it feeds largely on grasshoppers, beetles and lizards. On sandy commons, Kestrel pellets may be found formed entirely of the glossy, blue-black, very indigestible wing-cases of dor-beetles.

WOODCOCK
Scolopax rusticola

This large relative of the Snipe is the only bird in the big family of waders to have adapted completely to woodlands. In the winter it may be flushed from a damp hollow or rivulet in beech, oak or mixed woods. It occasionally calls '*fixt*' on rising, but it usually rises silently and, like a partridge, very suddenly from almost underfoot. It weaves away, 'jinking' from side to side, the manoeuvre which makes it hard even for a good shot to hit. As it flies it shows red-brown at each side of its fanned tail, then, when out of range of shot, clear of the trees, it may circle over the wood, a tubby bird with its long bill prominent, at a downward angle, and with broad wings. Woodcock are seen best when they circle their large territory at remarkably regular intervals towards dusk and at dawn. This peculiar flight is called 'roding' and occurs from March to July. The bird flies well above the trees with a slow wing-beat and every now and again it hesitates and gives a croaking call before or after a high pitched double note which carries far. The combined call is '*tissick, tissick, grrrk-grrrk.*' Woodcock feed mostly at dusk and dawn, probing soft mud for worms with their long bill, which has a sensitive expanded tip. They nest on the ground in bramble, bracken and general tangle under trees in oak, mixed or pine woods all over Britain. Nests should not be sought, for if disturbed before the eggs are hatched, the birds will desert them readily. If they are hatched, however, and the nest is disturbed even slightly, the parent birds carry the young away one by one held between the legs in a low flight. In October many Woodcock arrive here from northern Europe for the winter.

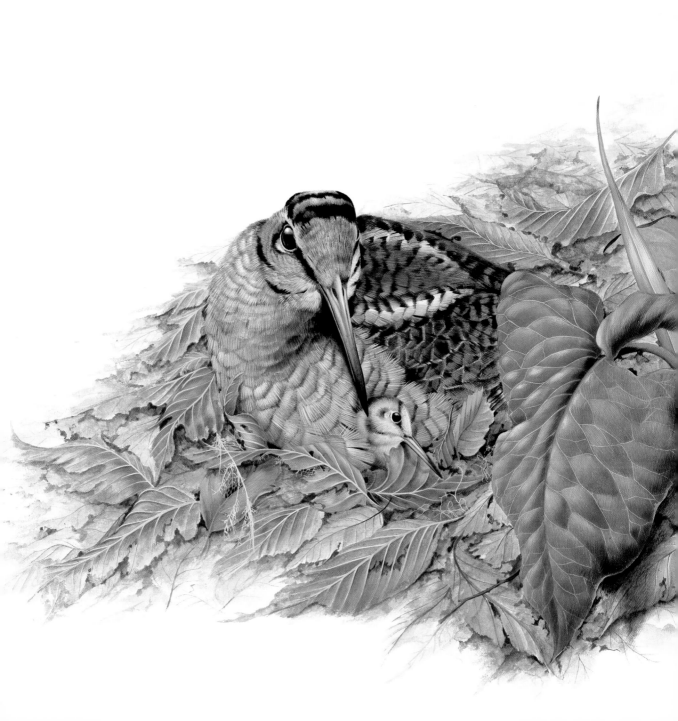

STOCK DOVE
Columba oenas

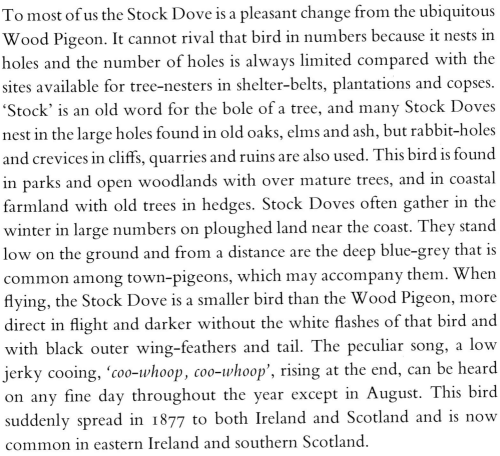

To most of us the Stock Dove is a pleasant change from the ubiquitous Wood Pigeon. It cannot rival that bird in numbers because it nests in holes and the number of holes is always limited compared with the sites available for tree-nesters in shelter-belts, plantations and copses. 'Stock' is an old word for the bole of a tree, and many Stock Doves nest in the large holes found in old oaks, elms and ash, but rabbit-holes and crevices in cliffs, quarries and ruins are also used. This bird is found in parks and open woodlands with over mature trees, and in coastal farmland with old trees in hedges. Stock Doves often gather in the winter in large numbers on ploughed land near the coast. They stand low on the ground and from a distance are the deep blue-grey that is common among town-pigeons, which may accompany them. When flying, the Stock Dove is a smaller bird than the Wood Pigeon, more direct in flight and darker without the white flashes of that bird and with black outer wing-feathers and tail. The peculiar song, a low jerky cooing, *'coo-whoop, coo-whoop'*, rising at the end, can be heard on any fine day throughout the year except in August. This bird suddenly spread in 1877 to both Ireland and Scotland and is now common in eastern Ireland and southern Scotland.

The bottom of the nesting cavity is usually lined with twigs, roots and dead leaves. The Stock Dove lays the standard Pigeon family clutch of two eggs. They are little longer than broad, a shiny creamy white, and take sixteen to eighteen days to hatch, being incubated by both parents. The yellowish buff young spend about twenty-eight days in the nest.

WOOD PIGEON
Columba palumbus

Pigeon and Dove are alternative names for all the birds in the family and the Wood Pigeon is often better known as the Ring Dove. In Scotland especially it is known as the Cushat or Cushy-doo. Very wary of man in the countryside, the Wood Pigeon will live in city parks and become so tame that it will feed from the hand. Pigeons have exceptionally strong back muscles for raising the wings. These not only make the Wood Pigeon a good bird to eat, but give it that rapid clattering take-off and the bouts of wing-clapping in the display flight. This can be seen at any time of year. A bird in level flight suddenly glides in a brief climb until it stalls, claps its wings, then dives out of the stall. Pigeons are also the only birds able to suck water into their bills and swallow it and can thus drink keeping their heads down where other birds must keep raising the head to tip the water down their open throats. Wood Pigeons may nest at any time of the year in city parks, but rural birds time their young for ripe grain in August. The nest structure is almost as casual as the timing and the few twigs just about hold the two eggs and young. Feeding the young is a strange process. The parents eat the grain and the lining of their crops swells and softens. The young bird, or 'squab' reaches into the crop with its bill and feeds on this lining as it is shed, forming what is called 'pigeon milk'. About eight million birds breed in Britain and with two young from each pair there are sixteen million birds by autumn, half of which must die if the population is to remain stable. In cold winters these starve from the shortage of clover and greens. Thus shooting has no effect on the numbers surviving, since until eight million have been shot, each death merely allows another to survive.

COLLARED DOVE
Streptopelia decaocto

When this bird is so constantly hooting at us and feeding on the bird-tray in the garden it is hard to remember that not so long ago it was unknown in Britain and at the beginning of the century there were none at all in Europe. The spread of the Collared Dove north and west across Europe is as remarkable as any phenomenon in the world of birds. It came to Istanbul from Asia Minor in about 1900 and spread very little further until after 1930, but by 1950 it was in Holland and the first pair bred in Britain in 1955 near Cromer in Norfolk. By 1964 there were estimated to be 19,000 birds in Britain, and by 1970 some 200,000, breeding in every county. At first it was found where Monterey cypress shelter-belts, common around our coasts, enclosed hen-runs, for that tree is very like the Italian cypress in Asia Minor, and the hen-runs provided easily found grain. Later it extended its choice to Lawson cypress, a tree found almost everywhere, particularly in towns. This enabled it to spread more widely and now it infests almost any conifers. There are two distinct colour forms of Collared Dove, one predominantly pale grey and the other sandy brown. Both forms show a conspicuous white tail, fanned when landing. In flight, the wings are broader than those of the Turtle Dove, more rounded at the tips and they have a slower, more even action giving a less dashing, slower flight, during which the bird makes a croaking, grating sort of single coo. The song may be heard throughout the year and is a hooting '*you-fool-you*', often a little yodelled as '*plu-ploo-plu*'. Two broods are usual but up to five are known. The nest is usually in an evergreen tree but may be in a deciduous one or even on a building.

TURTLE DOVE
Streptopelia turtur

This attractive little pigeon has acquired its English name from its soft, purring song, *'turr-turr'*, the Latin word 'turtur' meaning turtle. This almost drowsy call, redolent of high summer and hayfields, is first heard in the third week in April when the males arrive from southern Africa. From then until they return in September the birds may often be seen in pairs rising from puddles by roads in corn or meadowland with trees in the hedges, for they are thirsty birds. They rise rapidly showing golden backs and fanned tails prominently tipped white, broadest at the sides. In flight the Turtle Dove is remarkably like a wader, having slender, tapered wings with a fast, jerky action. Progress is swift and direct with rolling turns showing the white underside. These birds stay in pairs or single family groups until briefly before departure when a few hundred together may be found in large fields on low hills. When perched, which they often do on dead branches or on telegraph poles or wires, Turtle Doves are slim birds with markedly small heads and thin necks, soft pink breasts and a

patch of black barring on the side of the neck. Turtle Doves build their nests nearer the ground than other pigeons normally do and they like young plantations of conifers, as these give dense cover almost down to the ground. In young spruces the nest may be only one metre from the ground. It is also often in a tall dense hedge or thorn bush. The platform of fine twigs has a partial lining and two smooth white eggs are laid. Both parents incubate for fourteen days and there are usually two broods.

CUCKOO
Cuculus canorus

Although many people are unfamiliar with the appearance of the cuckoo, and might well mistake it for a hawk, everyone knows its easily imitated call, which we welcome each year on the bird's arrival, although it may become monotonous later on. Cuckoos also make a hoarse, cackling '*kwowowo*' and the hen has a chuckling note rather like bubbling water. Most of our cuckoos arrive from their winter home in Africa in mid-April, and quickly spread out over the country as far north as Shetland. Although it is a difficult species to census, its numbers are believed to have declined in the last twenty years or so. The female cuckoo patrols a fairly limited area while on the look-out for nests in which to lay her eggs, and each individual parasitises the same host-species, and lays eggs of the same type throughout her life. Over 50 foster-species have been recorded in Britain, but far the commonest are Meadow Pipit, Dunnock (pictured here), Reed Warbler and Pied Wagtail. They are rather small eggs for a bird of the cuckoo's size, but have a relatively thick shell. When ready to lay, the cuckoo swoops down to the chosen nest, quickly removes an egg in her bill, and lays her own in its place. The young cuckoo evicts any other chicks or eggs within a day or so of hatching, having a specially flattened back on which to lift them while it clambers backwards up to the rim of the nest. Baby cuckoos seem to be remarkably successful in their murderous activities, and the foster parents have to work hard to satisfy its rapacious appetite, and as it gets bigger and bigger may even have to stand on its back to feed it. The adult cuckoos, having no family to raise, are among the earliest of our summer migrants to leave, often in July or August, while the young birds can still be seen well into September.

36

LITTLE OWL
Athene noctua

Bird species introduced from another country tend either to fail or to succeed only too well and become an ineradicable pest. The Little Owl has taken the middle road. A pleasant addition to our birds it has found an unoccupied niche in the ecology, displacing or disturbing no other bird, spreading widely but nowhere becoming very numerous. The first introduction was unsuccessful but regular breeding began in Kent in 1896 and by 1933 it was breeding in every county south of Durham. It has spread very little since then and more recently has become scarce in some districts. The Little Owl is a bird of big old roadside trees in farmland, old parkland and open woods on heaths and commons. It is a dawn, daylight and dusk owl, not a nocturnal one and its plaintive, far-carrying call *'kiew'* is heard mainly by day, sometimes at regular intervals of about twenty minutes for many hours. As one form of song, the male and female may give a duet, making this call alternately. The Little Owl's favourite perch seems to be the ladder-rest on a telegraph-pole, but wires and fenceposts are also much used. It is a dumpy, compact bird when perched, with a fierce frown as the broad pale stripe above each eye bends down to join over the bill. In flight it looks like a short, blunt almost tail-less Mistle Thrush bounding like a woodpecker on short round wings. The diet is mainly beetles and other large insects and small mammals, but it will also eat earthworms, snails and minnows, and, in spring, small birds. Three to five white eggs are laid in a whole in a tree, cliff, quarry or ruin or sometimes a rabbit-hole. Only the female sits and usually only a single brood is raised.

TAWNY OWL
Strix aluco

This bird has three common names in equal usage and appears in many books as the Wood or Brown Owl. It is by far the most widespread and numerous owl in Britain but it has never spread to Ireland. It is the owl of city gardens and parks and of the suburbs and town centres. Its long, loud, slightly quavering hoot in B flat is the note commonly regarded as the standard noise for all owls. This is the song and is most heard after dark from January to June, but may be heard at any time of the year and also sometimes in the middle of the day, particularly in deep wooded valleys in Scotland. The call is heard even more frequently and is the eerie *'e-wick'* which may frighten some who are unused to night walks. It is most used by the female but the male will sometimes call, just as the female may hoot. A medley of similar calls issues from the young just out of the nest, but nestlings are often found pushed out prematurely and they pop corks splendidly. They should be left where they are for the parents to find. This owl is very nocturnal and is only seen on the wing in daylight when it has been flushed from its roost in an ivy-covered tree or a yew or spruce and quickly attracts a noisy band of jays, tits, chaffinches and blackbirds which mob it from a safe distance. In flight it is a large bird richly mottled in brown, cream and grey, with very broad wings and blunt head. The nest may be in a tree in the old nest of another bird or a squirrel's drey, or in a hole or crevice in rocks or ruins. The eggs are large and almost spherical and off-white. Only the female sits, starting when the first of about four eggs is laid and needing twenty-nine days before hatching starts.

GREEN WOODPECKER
Picus viridis

The Green Woodpecker, Yaffle, Rainbird or Popinjay has plenty of other names, mostly deriving from the old belief that its call presages rain. The largest of our woodpeckers, it is fairly common in suitably wooded areas south of the Pennines but infrequent north to the Lakes and since about 1950 in Dumfriesshire and around Dunkeld in Perthshire. It inhabits open woodland, parks, wooded heaths and gardens, and grazing land with trees in hedges and copses. It has become largely a ground-feeder, with a particular fondness for the yellow ant, which it extracts from anthill passages by insinuating its long, supple, sticky-ended tongue. It finds these mainly in rough grass but it also frequently searches mown lawns – where it looks out of place, a big colourful bird hopping about awkwardly and sitting back on its tail with its bill raised. Relying so much on the ground for its food the Green Woodpecker suffered much more serious loss to its numbers in the winter 1962–3 than did its tree-feeding relatives. The male plumage differs from the female only in the crimson in the moustachial stripes and rather brighter general colours, but both sexes show a conspicuous bright yellow rump as they fly away. This is the origin of many a 'Golden Oriole' sighting. The winter call is '*cheff-cheff-cheff*', a muted version of the longer, loud 'yaffling' spring call which rings out like a wild laugh. The nest-hole, pecked out by single blows, turns downwards for 30–40cm at the bottom of which four or five eggs are laid on a few chips of wood and are incubated by both birds for eighteen days.

43

GREAT SPOTTED WOODPECKER
Dendrocopos major

This handsome woodpecker is the most numerous and widespread of its family, now found well north of Inverness. It needs only a few birch or some beech with decaying branches to be at home in parks or gardens near towns, or pine and larch in the mountains. It also likes ash and oakwoods. It is very fond of fat and of nuts and it swoops down in the garden to scare other birds away from these and feeds watchfully but in full view of the house or at the window. This is a fairly recent change and it has also adopted the less pleasing habit of chiselling out the entrance hole of nest-boxes to reach in and eat the young. In woods of Scots or Corsican pine the Great Spotted Woodpecker will carry great quantities of cones to a favoured perch where it pecks out the seeds. It drops the cones until there is a large pile left below, or on the tree-stump which is often used for this purpose. The flight, as in other woodpeckers, is very dipping, alternately rising with a short burst of stiff-winged audible strokes and falling with the wings closed. It is a strong, fast flier freely traversing quite long distances and in spring showing its paces in frequent noisy chasings through the tree-tops accompanied by furious chittering calls. These are a variety of noises like '*wrrrrk-wrrrk*' and the normal contact call, a loud, positive '*tchik!*' which is often heard from a bird perched high in a tree. The song, from January to May, is an abrupt loud drumming made by hammering the bill against resonant timber. Both birds bore a nest-hole in a tree and incubate the five or so glossy white eggs.

LESSER SPOTTED WOODPECKER

Dendrocopos minor

This Robin-sized little bird is the least frequent of the three wood-peckers even within its limited range. Its habits also make it much less likely to be seen. It ranges north almost to Scotland but is mainly a bird of the midlands and south. It has not yet shown interest in nut-bags or other food put out for birds, and visits gardens only in the course of working through fruit-trees. For much of the year it feeds high in the tree-canopy and is little seen. In the winter it joins the large bands of roving Tits, Treecreepers and Nuthatches, and can be distin-guished by its more bounding flight when the flock streams across a ride or clearing. It is found in open woods, on commons with birch, parkland with old trees and in waterside alders. The only easy signs of this bird's presence are its call, a rapid '*pee-pee-pee,*' and its drumming song, but these are sparingly used. The call is heard mostly in late autumn and the song from February to May but with only a few days of intensive singing, often in early May. The drumming is mechani-cal, not vocal, and is in longer, softer and more even bursts than those of the Great Spotted Woodpecker, not fading rapidly. Apart from the big difference in size between these two, the Lesser differs in lacking red under the tail and in having stripes across its back. A single brood of about five young is raised in a hole bored by both parents in a decaying branch or small bole. The male incubates the eggs by night, the female taking the day's duty.

WRYNECK
Jynx torquilla

This aberrant member of the woodpecker family has now withdrawn as a breeding bird from southern England, but true to its eccentric style it has started breeding in northern Scotland for the first time. It has decreased in numbers in most of western Europe since 1900 for unknown reasons. Until then it bred in almost every county in Britain and was commonly known as the Cuckoo's Mate because it arrived at the same time as that other eccentric bird, in mid-April. The last nestings in the south were on heaths of pine and birch, the same habitat that they are now colonising in Strathspey, but the earlier haunts were parkland and open woods with old timber. The Wryneck is a regular migrant passing south along the east coast in the autumn, when it may be seen clinging to fence-posts in coastal marshes and fields. Seen thus, from the back it is a rich brown and black bird barred and streaked with grey. It is only marginally bigger than a sparrow. The Wryneck's song has the peculiar tone of voice of a woodpecker. It is a loud, measured '*kway-kway-kway . . .*' and sounds as it if were hard work, the song tailing away at the end as though the effort to continue were too great. When disturbed on the nest, which is in a hole or cavity fairly low in a tree, wall or bank, the bird weaves its head about and hisses like a snake. The English name, most European language names and the Latin adjective 'torquilla' are derived from this twisting of the neck. Usually only one clutch of about eight dull white eggs is laid and is incubated mainly by the female.

PIED WAGTAIL
Motacilla alba

The Pied Wagtails show a bewildering variety of plumages. The cock differs from the hen; both change for the winter; in autumn both have various partial moult plumages and the juveniles have their own. In addition, the Continental form of Pied Wagtail passes through and that has its own variations. This latter form, the White Wagtail, is scarcely distinguishable among the confusion of plumages in autumn but a cock bird seen in May running along the shore of a lake or reservoir or by the tide-line of a sandy bay is quite distinct. Where the Pied Wagtail has black continued from across the back to the throat, isolating the white face patch, the White has black only on the throat; the white of the face joins that of the underside, and the back is silvery grey. It is a more graceful slender bird, more active and more vocal. The Pied Wagtail is found around ponds and lakes and waterside meadows but is equally at home in big gardens with mown lawns, and around farms well away from water. In some villages of drystone houses in Wales and Cumbria it almost replaces the House Sparrow. It nests in holes in walls, thatched roofs, banks or cliffs or in drainpipes or old nests of other birds. The female builds the nest of stems, leaves, roots and moss. She lines it with hair, feathers and wool and lays five greyish eggs finely freckled grey-brown. The call, much used in the steeply dipping flight and from a perch or the ground, is a loud '*chissick*'. The song is sporadic throughout the year except in August and December. It is a medley of the call and loud twitters often given as the bird chases insects on a lawn. Pied Wagtails gather in the autumn from wide areas to large roosts. These are usually in reed-beds but in some regions hundreds of birds crowd into glasshouses or glass-roofed stations and in Dublin some two thousand roost in three plane trees in the centre of O'Connell Street, the busiest place in the city.

WAXWING
Bombycilla garrulus

The Waxwing gets its name from the scarlet tips on the inner wing-feathers which have wax-like knobs. These are less seen in flight than the small white wing-bar, the grey rump and the yellow tip to the tail. They have the same size, build and flocking habits as Starlings, so in flight when the crest does not show it is handy that they distinguish themselves by frequent use of a weak, sibilant '*srrr-r-r-ee*' call. They breed in northern Scandinavia and Siberia, laying one clutch of glossy pale blue eggs in a nest of twigs, lichen and moss. Every winter small parties arrive on our eastern coasts, but periodically, when the berry crops fail in Scandinavia, large numbers come and then they spread to the south and west in flocks of fifty to two hundred or so. At first they feed mainly on hawthorn berries and rose hips. When these are exhausted the flocks break up into smaller groups of a dozen to fifty birds and invade town gardens. Here they find the masses of berries on cotoneasters and firethorns that are little eaten by other birds, and the fruit of various flowering trees, often where other birds are too shy to feed. The Waxwing will feed happily in busy main streets, where tame birds with red crests arouse the interest of some who never would notice another bird. Feeding quietly close at hand they show well the soft, sleek silky plumage which is peculiar to them.

GARDEN WARBLER
Sylvia borin

This close relative of the Blackcap is a very dull bird to look at, a brown and buff nonentity, but it makes up for this by its glorious song. This is a loud and long warbling of rich notes, some of them throaty and deep and some higher and clear, with no set pattern. It differs from that of the Blackcap, which may be heard in the same places, in its greater length, deepness of some notes, more throaty voice and the lack of a final, clear high whistled phrase. Some songs include mimicry, and perversely this can include the final phrase of Blackcap song but does not usually end with it. The singing starts when the male birds arrive in the fourth week of April and ends in mid-July. At first singing is intensive and in a twenty minute period more than ten minutes can be spent in actual song. The Garden Warbler is not well named as few gardens contain enough thorn-scrub or woodland edge and young plantation for it, and commons, thickets and newly planted forests are its haunts. It is locally common in such places, as far north as central Scotland, but numbers fluctuate from year to year quite widely. After July, these birds are secretive and their 'shack-shack' call may be the only sign of their presence until they return to central Africa in mid September. Both birds build the nest, quite a large one of dry grass and moss, low in a bush or in herbage, but the cock builds a few more which are not used, as if to show he can manage without help. Both birds also incubate the four or five glossy eggs, which are variable in colour. They may be white or pink, green or buff, sparsely or densely blotched or speckled browns, reds and grey.

BLACKCAP
Sylvia atricapilla

The Blackcap spends the winter no farther south than around the Mediterranean Sea, so it is one of the first warblers to return in the spring. Early arrivals may be here in the last few days of March. Recently a number of them, mostly females and probably from Scandinavia, have wintered in southern England, where they are seen mostly at bird-tables. The females have trim little caps of chocolate brown in place of the black on the males. They arrive later and each is attracted to the territory of a male by his persistent singing. The song is a beautiful warbling and whistling, starting quietly with low warblings and becoming richer and louder until it abruptly rises to a clear whistling which ends with a set phrase, either rising or falling. Later in the season the preliminary warblings are shortened and the last songs which are heard around the end of July are only the final whistling. The call is a pebble-clashing 'tak-tak'. In most years this is a numerous bird in its habitats of woodland edge, clearings with brambles, scrub and bushes. It will breed in semi-suburban gardens where these still include areas of unused scrub but is driven away by the division of gardens and the infilling by houses that follows. Both parents build the nest which is clear of the ground in a bush or the sprouts and suckers of a tree. It is a small, neat cup of dead grass, roots, wool and down and is lined with fine grasses and hair. The eggs are usually five in number and variably pinkish, buff or white and speckled or blotched. They are incubated by both parents. Birds returning in the autumn frequent more open, bushy places and hedges and their presence may often be known only by their call.

WILLOW WARBLER
Phylloscopus trochilus

The Willow Warbler is probably the most numerous bird in the country during the summer as it is found almost everywhere that has long grass and bushes or trees and is especially common throughout the birch-clad hills of Wales and Scotland. The name is misleading as this is more a bird of birch, oak, hazel or hawthorn than of willows, though when first arrived from Central Africa in the last few days of March it will often be near water, in sallow and other willows. The song, heard almost continually until July, is a short sequence of clear notes descending in pitch and fading away but often reviving for a second descent. It is unhurried, lilting and, in a quiet way, very beautiful. The call-note, heard mainly in the autumn is an occasional feeble '*phor-wit*', more disyllabic than that of the Chiffchaff. Most warblers like to bathe in puddles and the Willow Warbler is small enough to use the dew or rain held in a big leaf. It will also hawk for flies over a grassy area darting out from and returning to bushes. The female builds the domed nest in long grass under a bush or in low cover, from moss, grass and bark lined with fine stems and feathers. There are six or seven very small glossy white eggs, lightly speckled reddish-brown. The female alone incubates, but the young are fed by both parents. The food given is small caterpillars. In the autumn Willow Warblers will eat elderberries and currants while in the spring the adults eat aphids, spiders and a wide variety of small beetles and flies. Immense numbers from more northern countries pass through in September and early October but, unlike Chiffchaffs in autumn, these very rarely sing.

CHIFFCHAFF
Phylloscopus collybita

The Chiffchaff is very similar in size and plumage to the Willow Warbler but is a little more brown and less clearly coloured, while in spring its legs are nearly black and those of the Willow Warbler are pale brown. A few Chiffchaffs now spend the winter in England and are seen around gardens and on bird-tables rather than in the open country. The main wintering area is around the Mediterranean so this bird is among the first to return in spring, having a much shorter journey than species which come from Central Africa; it is usually here by mid March. Spring immigrants sing at once on arrival whereas wintering birds remain silent. The song is a somewhat hesitant '*chip-chop-chap-chep-chip . . .*' often preceded by a little 'fritter' note which becomes almost obstructive later in the season but is absent from the infrequent singing resumed in September. The Chiffchaff is common in scrub, copses, woodland edges and birch woods everywhere except in the far north of Scotland. In the autumn vast numbers pass slowly southwards, visiting gardens and city parks which are avoided at other times. There may be one catching flies from the same bush every day for a fortnight but ringing has shown that this could be thirty different birds. In the autumn Chiffchaffs can be very aggressive and will chase birds as big as Blackbirds. The call is a soft, plaintive '*phu-i?*' The female builds a domed nest of stems, dead leaves and moss usually just clear of the ground in long grass or in a dense bush.

WOOD WARBLER
Phylloscopus sibilatrix

The Wood Warbler is closely related to the other two 'leaf warblers', the Chiffchaff and Willow Warbler. It is, however, noticeably bigger than the other two, it arrives three weeks later than they do, and being very particular in its habitat it is far less common or widespread. It is also a brighter coloured bird, with clear yellow breast and bright white beneath. It is a bird of high woodlands of beech, oak or sometimes birch. It has been noticed that wherever Wood Warblers breed there is whortleberry somewhere beneath the trees. It is most numerous in the woods of sessile oak on the hillsides of Wales and western Scotland, and is scarce in eastern England from London to York. This bird has two different songs. When first arrived in late April it tends to sing mainly the shivering trill which sounds like a coin spinning on a plate until it settles. The bird's tail quivers in time with this '*tip-tip-tip-tiptiptiptrrrrree*'. The first part is often given in flight and the '*trrrree*' when it has landed. An inferior second song unfortunately predominates from late June until singing ceases in July. This is '*dee-ur, dee-ur, dee-ur*'. The call-note is a strong '*peu*' or '*deer*' and is little used after breeding when the families move into the tree canopies and are hard to see. Even on migration, Wood Warblers are not often seen away from their breeding grounds. The female builds a domed nest of bracken, grass and dead leaves in a small hollow or amongst the small areas of low cover found in the woods it frequents, and lays six or seven eggs. These are glossy white much speckled with purplish-brown and there is usually only one clutch.

GOLDCREST
Regulus regulus

In winter just before dusk but after other small birds have gone to roost, a persistent '*seer-seer-seer*' comes from the Goldcrest, the smallest of them all. Each weighs but 5gm so it takes five to make an ounce. Such tiny birds suffer heavy losses in long, hard frosts and make good their numbers rapidly by raising large families. With two broods of ten young each season, one pair of Goldcrests could have thirteen tons of progeny in six years and a million tons in eleven years. In 1976, after thirteen mild winters, Goldcrests are everywhere, overflowing from their favourite spruce-woods into mixed woods, copses and gardens even near towns where they like the Lawson cypresses and churchyard yews, and into beechwoods and tall hedgerows. They sing a little in the autumn and winter but with great intensity from March to July when plantations of spruce, Douglas fir and hemlock are almost loud with the little song. It is a thin, high and rhythmic '*dee-diddle-dee-diddle-de-diddle-dee, dee-dee-dee*' usually ended with rapid but good

64

mimicry of a note or two of Blue, Coal or Marsh Tit. Although so thin and slight this song carries quite well and can be heard above the noise of passing traffic. The bird is indifferent to people in its woods or in gardens and will work through raspberry canes, for example, while they are being pruned. It will hover like a humming-bird on the outside of a holly bush. In different lights a Goldcrest can appear largely pale brown, pale yellow or mossy green. The female has a yellow crown-stripe where the male has orange. The nest is a deep cup of moss, lichen and spiders' web slung closely beneath and towards the tip of the branch of a conifer.

SPOTTED FLYCATCHER
Muscicapa striata

This flycatcher has a spotted plumage only when juvenile, and the Latin *striata* describes the adult better. This has pale greenish-brown wandering striations each side of the breast and along the flanks. Spotted Flycatchers reach this country from tropical Africa remarkably regularly on or very near May 6th and stay until the end of September. They like grazed parkland with old trees, for here the cattle attract insects and also browse the lower branches, leaving both a clear space for flight and a number of stubs on which the bird perches. Churchyards also tend to have shady trees kept clear of a ground rich in plants attracting insects and are relatively undisturbed. The Common Lime is the favourite tree, frequent in parks and churchyards and often bearing dense sprouts well up the bole. It is in these sprouts that this bird nests in the central parks of London: hey have spread into them since the cleaner air has allowed more insect life. The Spotted Flycatcher is usually seen either perched, sitting upright and showing its silky white breast, or on its dashing sally to catch an insect. To do this it darts out showing its narrow pale brown wings and performs an aerial dance around the victim, who is understandably unable to decide where to flee and is caught with an audible snap of the bill. The flycatcher then returns to the same perch, on a tree, fence-post or wire. The call is a husky '*tzeek*'. A short squeaky song '*zuk-zuk-zz-chaa*' is mainly confined to May. The nest is in any hollow or crevice, on a ledge over a door or in a creeper about 2–4m from the ground. If a house window is kept open a nest may be built on top of a cupboard indoors. It is a fine cup of feathers, spiders' web, hair and leaves on a large platform of the same materials and grass.

PIED FLYCATCHER
Ficedula hypoleuca

The Pied Flycatcher is much less seen than the flashing black and white plumage of the cock seems to warrant. This is because of its patchy distribution, its change of plumage and its habits. It is found where oak and ash are beside fast-flowing but moderately large streams and in hillside woods of sessile oak. These requirements limit the bird to the lower parts of the Pennine Hills from Derbyshire to Northumberland, to the Lake District and to central and northern Wales. A few breed by streams in Perthshire and near Exmoor and a number in the Forest of Dean, where they were found only when they occupied numbers of nest-boxes intended for a study of the tits. The hen is brown and white and may be overlooked as a Chaffinch. The cock is similar before the end of the breeding season and a few are brown and white while breeding. When the young leave the nest the families retire to the tree canopies and are little seen. Before this, insects are caught on the wing in the course of flight from one perch to another. The call is a clear '*phuweet*' and the song, which is frequent only in May and ceases by July, is a cheerful short phrase like '*tree-tree-tree-tui-tui-tree*' or '*tree-tree-sitroo-sitroo*'. The female builds a nest of strips of bark, grass, leaves, moss and lichen and lays a single clutch of smooth pale blue eggs. She incubates them while fed by the male for 13 days. The cock birds arrive in early April. A few which pass through to Scandinavia stay for a day or two in early May in places far from our breeding areas and may occur in a city park or on a golf-course. In the autumn large numbers arrive on the east coast but they travel south along the coast and are rarely seen inland.

REDSTART
Phoenicurus phoenicurus

On its arrival here at the beginning of April, the cock Redstart is a little flash of silver, black and fiery orange-red singing from a succession of high perches and flirting its tail. The song, a measured '*tree-tree-tree*' introducing a rapid medley of warbling, usually ends with one or more calls or songs of other birds reproduced with great accuracy. The Tree Pipit's song and woodpecker calls are easily recognised but the scolding of the Whitethroat followed instantly by a phrase of the Garden Warbler's song is easily overlooked as random warbling. Seventeen different items of mimicry were noted in the repertoire of one Redstart. They require various but definite habitats. In the western hills they are found in the woods of sessile oak with the Pied Flycatcher and in the Pennine ashwoods similarly, but they range beyond these to the north-eastern stone-wall country by sycamore-lined roads. In the south and east they are found in old oaks, young birch and, on the heaths, in clumps of old Scots Pine. The call is a rather sharp '*phui*' or '*chip-chip-phui*' and is aggravatingly like the calls of both the Pied Flycatcher and the Nightingale, which share some of the same habitats. The female builds a nest in a tree-stump, a hole high in a tree or low in a stone wall, making a loose cup of dead grass and leaves, moss and bark fibres, and lines it with hair and feathers. She lays six or seven smooth glossy light blue eggs and incubates them herself. After helping to feed the second brood, the male loses his bright plumage and is warm brown like the female. They both still have the red tail and rump and these are the only conspicuous signs of the large numbers of migrants passing south in September, as they dart into hedges and bushes.

ROBIN
Erithacus rubecula

Male and female Robins look exactly alike and in the winter each defends its own territory by song and by battle. It is understandable therefore that long ago Robin Redbreast was always a male, 'Cock Robin', and that he should have a mate who must be 'Jenny Wren'. We do not call the Wren 'the Jenny' but we do, for some reason, call the Redbreast 'the Robin'. In Britain the Robin is peculiarly confiding and attracted to man. In the winter one may fly out of some forest cover to land hopefully at the feet of a passer-by while suburban and country garden Robins keep a close eye on all operations in their garden. When offered a fat grub from the digging, a Robin will often ignore it but dart in to seize an invisible insect right by the gardener's boot. Robins enter houses freely to feed on the inside window-sill and to tease fibres from the doormat for their nest. The female builds this, often in a frenzied rush, piling up old leaves in the corner of a shelf so that unless the door be kept firmly shut she will have a large nest in two or three days. She also builds in sheds, in crevices in walls, and in old pans or kettles under a bush. She lays five or six white eggs with pale brown speckles. Juvenile Robins are brown with pale spots all over. The orange breast begins to appear before the young are independent. On adult birds the orange extends over the face and across the forehead, a fact which has not yet been appreciated by the artists of too many Christmas cards and childrens' books. The call, usually denoting slight annoyance is '*tic*' and for mobbing owls or mild alarm several are run together. For real alarm, there is a keening '*tseek*'. The song of the female and of the male in winter is a plaintive series of whistlings and rippling, dying away trills with many discordant notes. The spring song, given by the male usually from a perch ten to twenty metres up in a tree, is a challenging whistling and warbling with more positive trills ending sharply.

NIGHTINGALE
Luscinia megarhynchos

From its arrival in mid-April until early June, the Nightingale sings at all times of day and night except when one takes a party to hear it. Overcast and windy weather inhibits song to some extent and in many years recently April and May have been dull with cold winds and the song has been sporadic. Several other birds sing at night, notably the Woodlark, Reed Warbler and disturbed Robins and Dunnocks, but none has a song at all like that of the Nightingale. Many people make much of preferring the Blackbird's song but as a performance the Nightingale's song is incomparably the finest heard here. None other has the range of quality, speeds, pitch and volume. A thin, high note is drawn out more and more slowly until a sudden burst of rich deep 'jugging' follows, audible more than half a mile away, then loud warbles lead to a hard, rapid rattle which ends in a sharp, whistled flourish. The call-note is a sharp '*phweet*' and is often followed by a scolding croak during the nesting period. Nightingales are locally frequent east of a line from Exeter to The Wash, but the bushy commons, oak copses and chestnut coppice that they live in are in this region endangered by fire, disturbance by people and dogs and by change of land-use, even where they survive by-passes and motorways which are aimed through the least populated parts. Their best refuge now is the dense stands of young trees in forests, conifer or broad-leaved. The female builds a nest in long grass under a bush, from dead grass and oak-leaves and lays four or five olive-brown eggs. In early autumn some Nightingales pass through and are seen flying low into coastal bushes showing red brown rumps and tails like the Redstart's but darker.

BLACKBIRD
Turdus merula

In the winter the Blackbird is probably the most numerous and widespread bird in this country. Hardly a scrap of cover is without its Blackbird, from mountain-top gully to sand-dune hollow and from deep forest to city square. In shape and habits the Blackbird is evidently one of the large thrushes and this is shown also in the golden-spotted juveniles and in the speckled grey throat and breast of the adult female. Male Blackbirds in gardens become highly disreputable in the summer, losing their gloss and often their tails as well and becoming bald on the head, face and neck until they moult in autumn. The flight-note is a thin quavering '*tseesk*' which is heard from migrants passing over on autumn nights as well as during the short low flights into the bottom of a bush which are as much as it normally does. Mild alarm causes a '*chook-chook*' while somewhat greater alarm causes a loud '*pink, pink*'. But this neurotic bird frequently shows even greater alarm and then the '*pink*'s become a long clattering as it flies away, dying down as it lands. The 'pink' note is also used persistently as the Blackbird fusses around the outskirts of a party of other birds mobbing an owl, and in long sequences before the bird goes to roost. The same note accompanies the strange territorial rites when six or seven cock birds line a hedge-top, scolding, then drop on to the lawn and hop in line ahead, one moving at a time in short crouching rushes ending with raising the head and fanning the tail. Song begins in late January and is the sustained background to the dawn chorus in April and May. It is a varied warbling and whistling, partly in musical intervals, even with chance snatches of known tunes, in short phrases, some of them squeaky. The hen builds a big nest of stems, grass and leaves with mud and lined with fine grasses, in any bush, tree or shed. The five eggs are glossy light blue and finely speckled.

FIELDFARE · REDWING
Turdus pilaris · Turdus iliacus

The Fieldfare and Redwing are the more sociable, colourful and vocal northern migratory equivalents of the Mistle Thrush and Song Thrush. They spend the winter in meadows and playing-fields with surrounding trees and when they are disturbed they fly into the crowns of the trees. The Fieldfare flocks arrive in October and at first are conspicuous and noisy around bushes and hedges. They seem to be black and white but at closer range they show pale grey rumps, dark brown tails and wings, and blueish heads while the very white underside shades to a brown breast. The usual call is a husky '*cheeyok-chok-chok*' constantly heard from flocks on the move by day and occasionally heard from the night sky. When a flock is flushed and takes to the trees one or more birds will make a bugling call like '*kyee-owk*'. In late March birds may gather in a single tree in the evening and give a long loud chorus of chattering and some clearer notes and then abruptly all fall silent. The Fieldfare breeds in northern Europe but there is a colony in the Alps and a few now breed in northern Scotland. They come into gardens for fallen or unpicked apples in November and again later if there is a severe spell of frost and snow. The Redwing is the first bird to suffer in such weather and they then invade town gardens for berries, but many die. They keep at other times to playing-fields and meadows until dusk when they assemble noisily to roost in rhododendrons or dense shrubberies. They call with a '*took-took-took*', chackering notes and a thin, high '*tzeenk*' and this last, slightly metallic piping note is the one heard on October nights from passing flocks. In March they assemble on sunny mornings for choruses of quiet musical phrases but the song, heard now from an increasing colony breeding in northern Scotland, is a loud and clear one. The broad cream stripe on the head and the bright red stripe along the flanks show well on the birds as they hop, head to wind, feeding in the fields.

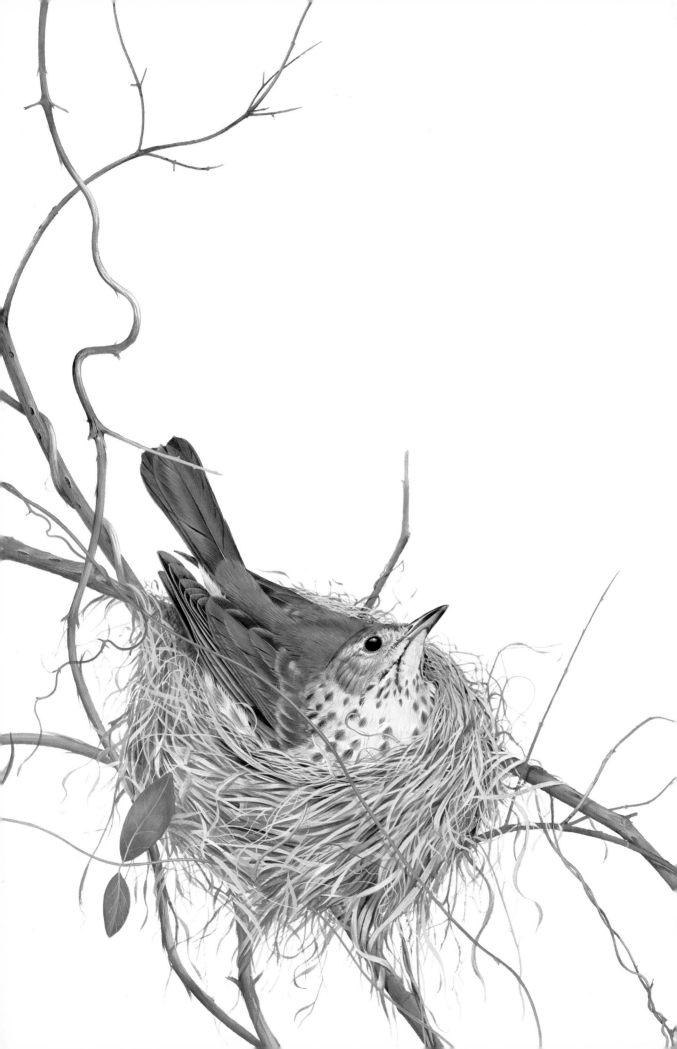

SONG THRUSH
Turdus philomelos

The Song Thrush is a timid bird yet it is confiding. It yields to every bird except the Dunnock at a feeding-place but it may hop serenely through the sitting-room in its quest for currants. It will also sit on a nest in scant cover by a busy pathway. It is therefore a common bird in small gardens with a minimum of cover and feeds on lawns and flower-beds. Around midsummer the big garden snail suddenly becomes the favourite meal for a few weeks and the thrush is heard breaking their shells against a convenient stone or brick. These anvils are soon surrounded by fragments of snail shells. In flight the Song Thrush is most often seen as a warm brown bird dashing into low cover with a sharp '*tissk*' call. It uses a similar, shorter '*tsik*' when it needs more currants. Supplied with these to feed its young, this bird shows no restraint and when eight are crammed into its bill it stabs at a ninth and one falls off. This has to be gathered and another falls off and much time is wasted before the bird admits defeat. In October the cock starts to sing especially at dusk when it cannot be feeding, but also as the sun is sinking so that to keep in its rays it climbs to successively higher perches. The song is a long series of clearly defined phrases of great variety each usually repeated one to five or more times. Some phrases are in general use, like '*did-he-do-it, did-he-do-it*', '*victor! victor!*' and a falling '*clikitit*' but some are individual. Some are mimicry, like the '*tui-tui-tui*' of the Nuthatch. The female builds the nest in a bush, often in a clipped hedge, or in a cypress or spruce with living branches low down. She makes a cup of grass, roots and moss and lines it with mud and rotted wood smoothed and shaped with her breast. She lays and incubates about five smooth blue eggs lightly speckled or blotched dark brown.

81

MISTLE THRUSH
Turdus viscivorus

Blustery November gales bringing rain from the south-west provoke the Mistle Thrush into song. From a high, exposed perch, head to wind it shouts its short, skirling phrases with little variation, showing a monotony which distinguishes them from those of the Blackbird's song which is of a similar form. Rising to a challenge is characteristic of the Mistle Thrush and during nesting time any bird, regardless of size may be driven from his territory, pursued with an aggressive rattling churr. Magpies and Carrion Crows are, very wisely, particularly disliked and will be harried relentlessly, while a Sparrowhawk unwittingly passing may be brought down and a man too close to the nest may be attacked. In the autumn a Mistle Thrush may appropriate a well-berried yew and spend the day trying to defend it from Song Thrushes and Blackbirds who had been unaware of its ownership. In August family parties move to the hills and unite into flocks of a hundred or two and feed on the rowan berries, returning in October. Then pairs will come into suburban gardens where they eat large scraps on the bird-table but prefer sultanas. The Mistle Thrush flies in easy, shallow waves and when landing it shows a small white patch each side of the tip of the tail. It forages much on mown lawns or on meadows with Song Thrushes, when it is seen to be a good size larger and a greyer brown without the warm red tones of the Song Thrush. Its spots are bigger, rounder and more uniformly spread with big ones along the flanks. The Mistle Thrush female builds the nest very early, usually in February, in a fork in a tree, and this is one of the few nests often found in a Sycamore. It is a large cup of grass, moss, leaves and earth. There are two broods of about five eggs each. The eggs are glossy pale blue evenly spotted with reddish-purple.

82

LONGTAILED TIT
Aegithalos caudatus

The Longtailed Tit is odd man out among the tits not only in the tail but in the pink, black and white colouring and in building its nest out in the open. Some consider it the solitary member of a separate family. This bird is no bigger than a Goldcrest but has 6cm more tail. Its breeding rate is less than that of the Goldcrest as it raises only one brood, but it can even so recover rapidly from the big losses caused by a hard winter. After the many mild winters recently, it is now remarkably numerous and breeds in thickets of thorn, blackthorn or gorse, in hedges and shrubs in open woodland almost anywhere. In the winter they form flocks, a family party of six to twelve or groups of fifty or more. The larger flocks roam high woodland and join the big mixed tit and other small bird flocks briefly when passing the same way. In the last twenty years Longtailed Tits have become regular feeders at bird-tables in semi-suburban gardens and may visit one at the same time of day for weeks. Streaming from tree to tree the birds look like flying tadpoles and keep up a chorus of thin, high 'see-see-see' calls. When feeding they also use a soft rattling 'drrrr' and 'tup'. On a bird-table they hold their tails high so that many can crowd into a small space without any squabbling. Both birds build the nest, in March before the leaves give cover so that many of those in black-thorn are lost and a later nest is built, sometimes up to 15m from the ground in an oak. The egg-shaped nest consists of up to two thousand small feathers and of moss, held together by cobweb and covered with lichens. The cobweb keeps the nest together as it expands to hold the ten to twelve growing young.

85

COAL TIT

Parus ater

This is the brightest of the tits in everything except plumage. It is the most active, perky and vocal, with the most musical voice, and it is also the smallest. It flits on to a nut-cage, prises clear a large lump, flits away to hide it and is back within half a minute for another. Although the Coal Tit can be numerous in gardens in an area which is generally fairly well wooded, it is less a bird of gardens than of beechwoods, conifers and mixed woods. It visits gardens towards town centres only in winter. This bird is common nearly everywhere in Britain, whilst Ireland has its own form of Coal Tit in which the underparts of the adult retain the yellow colour of the juvenile and which has more penetrating call-notes. The Coal Tit uses some calls very like those of the other tits but is easily distinguished by its frequent use of clear, sharp notes like '*pweet*', '*peer*' and '*tse-peer*' and a very thin 'eeze-eeze' more like a Goldcrest. The song is a rapid, clear '*tuwee-tuwee-tuwee . . .*' at short intervals. The nest is built by the female in a hole in a bank, wall or tree-roots and is made of moss and spiders' web lined with hair and feathers. The eggs, about eight in number are white, sparsely freckled and blotched with purplish-red, and take 14–18 days to hatch, incubated by the female only. Very small birds like the Coal Tit suffer heavy mortality in long hard winters and build up their populations again rapidly in milder periods by raising large broods. Losses from cold were negligible between 1963 and 1975, when numbers of Coal Tits were at an unprecedentedly high level.

GREAT TIT
Parus major

This is distinctly the largest of the tits, and a boldly handsome bird in black, white, blue, green and yellow. In spring the cock is even more resplendent for the black on the head has a high gloss of metallic blue. He differs from the hen only in this and in the broader black band down his middle. When flying low, the Great Tit shows a nearly black tail with white outer feathers like a Chaffinch and unlike the other tits. When feeding, it shows a whitish area at the base of the crown but not a clearly defined stripe like the Coal Tit. The Great Tit is common in small numbers in woods, gardens, hedgerows and copses. In the autumn and winter it comes into town gardens and parks and is a regular feeder at nut-cages. Many also winter in beechwoods and feed partly on the nuts, while others join the large roving mixed flocks in oak and mixed woods. Although hardly a noisy bird, the Great Tit has a very large vocabulary and one diligent student has distinguished seventy-two different calls that may be used. The most frequent calls include a Chaffinch-like '*pink-pink-pink*', the '*see-see-see*' common to several of the tits, and when low in a bush, often a deep, husky '*zuzz-zuzz-zuzz*.' Another call in the autumn flocks is a rapid '*see-sawsee*'. The song, first heard in early January, is a somewhat rasping '*see-saw-see-saw . . .*' but odd variants are frequent and the bird is most easily recognised by the tone of its voice rather than by what it says. The female builds in any hole or crevice, usually not far from the ground and lays eight to thirteen purple-speckled white eggs.

BLUE TIT
Parus caeruleus

This is the most numerous and widespread of the tits and is found almost anywhere where there is good cover, from town gardens to reed-beds and salting edges. When a nut-cage is first filled in autumn, Coal Tits may for a while be dominant, but soon it is the Blue which is queuing up and twenty or so of them may be there. Ringing has shown that when no more than a dozen are seen at once there may well be a hundred and fifty actually coming to the food. The back, wings and tail of the Blue Tit are azure blue, so when it flies away it is seen as a completely blue bird and unlike any other tit. Seen from ahead, the white face is prominent with black behind it, a feature from which the bird is sometimes called the 'Nun'. The usual calls are a high pitched *'see-see-see'* and a rapid low churring but the song is much used from January until June and this is a clearly declaimed *'blue-blue-tititit'*. The nest is in a hole, almost anywhere – in the ground, a wall, pillar-box or lamp-post – and is built by the female from moss, grass, wool, hair, dead leaves and spiders' webs, and lined with feathers. About ten tiny white eggs speckled red or brown are laid and the female sits on them. In Britain this, like the other tits, has only a single brood. With the food supply for the young plentiful over a short period and with the safety that comes from nesting in holes, a single large brood taking a few more days to raise than a small brood, can yield more fledged young than two small ones over a longer span. The young are fed by both parents with thousands of greenfly and small caterpillars.

MARSH TIT
Parus palustris

WILLOW TIT
Parus montanus

These two small tits are so alike that the Willow Tit was distinguished as a native breeding bird only in 1888, the last common species to be discovered. There are several rather minor differences between these birds in their plumage but none is reliable at other than fairly close quarters and it is only by learning the clear differences between their notes first that these finer points can be used with confidence. Both species are frequent in woods and scrub and in hedgerows near woods, and in birch copses. In many parts, like the southern chalklands, the Willow Tit is locally dominant and in Cumbria and south Scotland it replaces the Marsh Tit. The best distinction is the usual call-notes, the Marsh Tit calling '*pitchou*' and '*chickadee-dee*' and the Willow Tit calling a very nasal '*jaaa*' or '*twit-twit-jaaa-jaaa-jaaa*' and a thin high '*eeze-eeze . . .*' The song of the Marsh Tit is a rapid '*dlipdlipdlip . . .*' and that of the Willow Tit '*dee-ur, dee-ur, dee-ur . . .*'. The least obscure difference in plumage is that the black cap of the Marsh Tit is shiny, neatly defined and small, not extending much on to the nape whereas that of the Willow Tit is dull, somewhat ragged and ill-defined and extends well down the nape. There is also a difference in build in that the Willow Tit, excavating as it does its nest-hole, has a strong stout neck which the Marsh Tit, nesting in natural holes in stumps or decaying trees, lacks. In both species the nest is made by the female and she alone incubates the six to nine eggs and is fed by the male during this time. Both species will feed on nut-cages in gardens in relatively lightly built-up areas.

NUTHATCH
Sitta europaea

The Nuthatch is a cheerful bird in manner and voice throughout the year and is neat and pretty in its plumage. It is oddly similar to the Kingfisher in build, beak and colouring although much less brilliant. The soft blue-grey of its back ends in a pattern of white on the tail. This is seen only when it fans its tail on landing or during display. It is never quiet for long, calling with clear, whistled notes, '*tui*' or '*tui-tui-tui*' as it runs about on the trunks and branches of old trees. The triple note is very like a pebble bouncing across ice. In the spring longer phrases are given as song, including a high '*pe-pe-pe-pe*' and a rapid trill but all the notes are in the same clear whistling voice. This makes the flight-note seem out of character as it is a tit-like '*tsssrrr*'. Holding its short tail well clear of the tree, the nuthatch can run up or down the boles equally well. Feeding at a nut-bag it much prefers to operate head downwards, extracting whole nuts and taking them away to be hidden in a crevice in the bark of a tree. Most oak trees have eaten-out nuts jammed in their bark which are the Nuthatch's work. This bird is frequent in old ash or beech woods and in oakwoods, in parkland and on commons with birch trees, throughout England and Wales but rarely occurs in Scotland and never in Ireland. In some places Nut-hatches will feed on the ground and come for crumbs. At others they may be seen on the ground only when collecting mud with which they plaster the interior of the nest-hole and reduce the size of the entrance. The male helps in this but the female does most of the nest building, making a loose cup of wood-chips, bark and dead leaves. She lays six to nine smooth white eggs, lightly speckled reddish, and incubates them herself, during which time she is fed by the male.

TREE-CREEPER
Certhia familiaris

It is necessary to know the call of the Tree-creeper to appreciate how common and widespread it is, for it is a small and inconspicuous bird. It is seen occasionally flying down to the base of a tree, usually to climb the bole on the side out of view, but otherwise needs looking for, climbing in a jerky way on trunks and branches well into the canopy. The calls are quavering thin notes, either a single '*tsirrr*' or a slow '*tseep, tseep*'. The song starts with these notes then, just as it is under way it stops with a flourish; '*tsee-tsee-tissi-see-swee-ip!*' The male sings all the year except in August. Tree-creepers inhabit old deciduous trees in parklands, woods and hedgerows and on commons, and in mixed woods. Small winter parties mixed with Goldcrests may roam the edges of conifer plantations. Most Tree-creepers seem now to roost in cavities they make in the fibrous spongy bark of Sequoia trees, for specimens of both the Coast Redwood and the Wellingtonia usually have many of these hollows on their sheltered side, marked by the white of the birds' droppings. In spring, pairs may chase rapidly among the boles of trees with a direct flight unlike the wavering and dipping normal progress. Both sexes help to build the nest in a crevice behind flaking bark or between the bole and a stem of ivy. They will use a bundle of twigs wired against the bole of a tree if natural sites are scarce. The cup is made of moss, grass, twigs and roots and is lined with feathers, shreds of bark and some wool. Two broods are usual, each of six smooth, matt white eggs finely speckled towards the broad end with pink. The female alone incubates the eggs but both parents feed the young.

97

WREN
Troglodytes troglodytes

There are fifty-nine true wrens in the world and fifty-eight of them are strictly confined to the Americas. The other one occurs in North America and in a broad band across most of Europe through Central Asia to Japan. This perky little bird with the upturned tail and loud song needs only a small refuge of undisturbed low cover. It finds this in stone walls and boulders high in the mountains; in scrub inshore of sand-dunes, in hedgerows, woods and large gardens and parks but rarely in suburban gardens. It is one of the first birds to move into conifer plantations when branches and tops from the first thinning give cover on the forest floor. The Wren flies low and in a direct line. With whirring wings and short rounded tail it looks like a large brown bumble-bee. The call is a hard '*trrr*' and when scolding or alarmed, the same note but longer is used, three or four together. The powerful song is a long series of trills connected by springy '*zicky-zicky*' passages, ending with a hard rattle and '*ke-zik*' and is sung freely throughout the year. To aid survival during long freezing nights, wrens roost packed into old nests. One bird-box was seen to be entered by sixty-eight birds for the night. The cock builds the exteriors of several nests in his territory and may install several different females in them in succession, the females adding the lining. The nests are large domes of leaves, moss and bracken and are lined with feathers. They are between a tree bole and an ivy stem or in a hole in a wall or bank. Each female lays a single clutch of five to eight tiny glossy white eggs minutely speckled at the broader end with black or red-brown. Wrens may often be seen running about in a mouse-like way around old walls, sheds, and frames, seeking spiders.

CHAFFINCH
Fringilla coelebs
BRAMBLING
Fringilla montifringilla

This is a pair of closely related finches of which the Brambling is the northern and eastern bird from Norway to eastern Siberia and the Chaffinch is the southern and western member. It ranges from Spain to Norway and the Black Sea. In Britain it is one of the most numerous of all birds and is found almost anywhere that has trees or bushes. At open air cafes it is as confiding as the House Sparrow feeding on the table-tops. In the winter flocks arrive from the Baltic states to inhabit open farmland. The females travel ahead and range further south so there are many flocks of males only, from which the name '*coelebs*' or bachelor, is derived. The flight-note is '*chup*' and the usual call is '*pink!*' from which we have the word 'finch'. The song is a cheerful descending rattle ending with a flourish which varies with the local dialect. The best singers end their songs with '*to-meet-you*' or '*pretty-dear*' but poor songs fade into '*che-ree*'. The nest is often rather exposed on the bough of a fruit-tree but it is well camouflaged with grey lichens and green moss. A few Bramblings nest in northern Scotland in some years but the big flocks arrive on the east coast in October. They settle in beechwoods and wooded farmland and small numbers appear in gardens near towns, where birds are fed. In flight Bramblings are known by their hard '*tuk-tuk-tuk*' note and when flushed from feeding on spent hop piles or beech-nuts they differ from the Chaffinches with them in showing a white rump but less white on the dark wings and tail.

GOLDFINCH
Carduelis carduelis

Among the old nouns of assembly for birds, the 'exultation' of larks and 'sedge' of Herons, none is a happier choice than a 'charm' of Goldfinches. These birds are lively, pretty and fairly confiding, with a musical voice. The flight-note is a light *'twicky-wick'* given with almost every bounce of the buoyant flight and at rest there are constant calls of *'twicky-wicket'* and *'fayee?'* The song is a rapid mixture of these notes with canary-like liquid twitters, given in flight or perched. The Goldfinch had become scarce by 1900 but is now common although numbers fluctuate. When numerous, the Goldfinch breeds in the outskirts of towns, mainly in Lawson cypresses and in cherry-trees. The female builds the nest of moss, lichens, grass, wool and plant down and lays about five glossy very pale blue eggs finely marked with purple or pink. Family parties gather to feed on the seeds of thistles, burdock and teasels; a field of chicory or a heap of spent hops at a nursery may attract several hundred birds. In the breeding season Goldfinches like railway cuttings, golf-courses, commons with gorse, and old orchards. They sing, often from telegraph wires, mostly from March to July but sometimes in October and February.

GREENFINCH
Carduelis chloris

SISKIN
Carduelis spinus

These two birds will compete for a place on a nut-bag, and the Greenfinch loses although it is much the larger bird. Eating a nut is a slow process for a Greenfinch as it only nibbles at it, and keeps stopping to threaten with open bill and half-opened wings adjacent tits and other Greenfinches. This is a sociable bird, breeding as well as feeding in groups. It likes to nest in Lawson cypresses and yews and so it is common in suburban gardens and churchyards. The contact and flight-calls are a pleasant *'checheche'* and a seasonal call heard from February until July is a droning, harsh *'dzweer'*. The song is rather canary-like, a mixture of these notes and longer trills, heard at its best when the bird gives it in a slow, level flight with the wings flapped slowly and deliberately.

The Siskin is a close relative of the Goldfinch and the Redpoll and is often in flocks with these in riverside alders. Its attention to nut-bags is a very recent change in its habits, perhaps associated with its spread to the south as a breeding bird. It has been noticed that red nut-bags attract Siskins more than those of other colours. Single birds or a pair flying for some distance give a clear *'tseeeoo'* call, but a flock going from one tree to the next flies in a tight bunch making a buzzing twitter. When feeding, the *'fayee?'* call is used as in all these small finches. The tiny nest is high in a conifer, towards the tip of a branch.

BULLFINCH
Pyrrhula pyrrhula

The Bullfinch has benefited from a change in its habits. Thirty years ago it was very shy, seen only as a departing flash of white rump and confined to thickets, overgrown hedges or larch woods at up to 700m above sea-level. It came to appreciate that man is dangerous only near fruit-trees, so it spread into quite built-up areas. Now numerous in semi-suburban gardens, Bullfinches will quietly disbud roadside trees in the full view of passers by. The normal food in winter is the seeds of ash, field maple and dock, with hawthorn buds. Ash and maple are irregular in fruiting and dock tends to be destroyed by weed-killing sprays. The female needs a richer diet than just hawthorn buds when she will soon be laying eggs so she turns to the buds of fruit-trees, Forsythia and other plants in the gardens she can now inhabit. Bullfinches mate for life and the pair stay close together, so the male comes too. They call to each other with a soft, piping '*pheep*' when feeding or in flight, and a good imitation of this note can bring the cock bird very near. The song can be heard in any month, but only just; it is so quiet that only one phrase is audible at a normal distance. This is a lilting '*phit-phit – phor-phor*'. The female builds a nest, a small cup of roots and hair on a platform of twigs, in a dense bush. She lays about five eggs which are pale glossy blue, heavily spotted brown around the broadest part. Parties of a dozen or more birds may gather in a big hedgerow or tall thicket in January or February.

HAWFINCH
Coccothraustes coccothraustes

To take anyone out to see a Hawfinch is like taking him to see a rainbow; it could be anywhere and it needs luck to succeed. Hawfinches like tall old trees, conifers and hardwoods mixed and some with dead tops. The major gardens and tree-collections are the most reliable places, from Bodnant in North Wales and Chatsworth in Derbyshire to Nymans and Wakehurst Place in Sussex, the National Pinetum at Bedgebury in Kent, and Windsor Great Park in Berkshire. In March the birds perch high and attract attention by their calls and song. The calls are a loud '*ptik!*' more explosive than the similar call of the Robin, and a '*tseeip*', and the song is merely these two notes run together with some twittering. At other times these extremely shy birds are seldom seen unless the notes are known, when they will be seen flying fairly high using either or both calls. Heavy looking birds, in flight they bound deeply and usually call at each bound. The big bill is noticeable, and daylight shows through the big white panel in each wing-feather and through the white at each side of the very short tail. Hawfinches are fond of the seeds of the hornbeam and flocks are sometimes found in Epping Forest where this tree is common, while single trees anywhere may have a bird or two feeding beneath, even on a road. At such times, the big pale blue bill and black bib are prominent and one may see the metallic blue-black feathers of the inner wing which have hatchet-shaped, broadened ends unique among our birds. Hawfinches have bred in Britain only since 1800 and have spread as far as south Scotland. Usually they lay only one brood of five bluish eggs, sparsely and irregularly scrawled and spotted.

REDPOLL
Carduelis flammea

This pretty little finch may visit any garden that has a birch tree, to feed on the seeds in the autumn and winter. There may be one pair or about twenty birds, but on commons and hillsides with many birches the flocks are often fifty or sixty strong. Even bigger flocks gather with Siskins in water-side alders from October until March. Redpolls hang on the slender twigs to feed, quietly teasing out the seeds when at various angles, their slender 'fishtail' tails projecting and the pale buff wing-bar and streaked flanks showing. In January they feed on the birch seed which is on the ground and then the red cap and neat black bib of the male can be seen well. Every now and again a '*fayee?*' call or a quiet '*jidgit*' is given, and before flying away a chorus of calls arises. The flock flies in a close group, bouncing merrily and calling '*jidgit*' in concert, circles and lands in another tree. This distinctive flight-note is heard from the birds arriving at the coast in autumn as they fly over, also from high flying birds inland. The song, often given during a circling, hesitant flight, is a series of flight-notes and a long quiet but hard rattle. The Redpoll has increased and spread greatly in recent years with the growth of young forestry plantations. It breeds in larch woods and also in birch or in thorns, sometimes even in small town parks and several nests may be in one bush. They are untidy small cups of fine twigs, grass and stems lined with plant down and feathers where the female alone incubates the five pale blue lightly speckled eggs.

TREE SPARROW
Passer montanus

The undoubted appeal of this bird to the birdwatcher is that it is not the House Sparrow, but a welcome change. Moreover in every way that the two differ it is the Tree Sparrow that is the superior bird. The sexes are alike and each has a fine chestnut crown and a neat black bib and is a brighter, cleaner bird than the House Sparrow. The face is white with an isolated patch of black behind the eye, making a pattern easily visible as the bird flies past. The Tree Sparrow has to be sought in rural areas and is rarely seen in a garden. Old trees, especially oak, ash and elm, in open woods, in hedgerows or as more isolated trees around fields near the coast are favoured for breeding, but in winter large flocks form in weedy fields and at sewage farms. Many of these birds are winter visitors whose passage above the coast is identifiable from their hard '*tk, tk*' flight-note. The ordinary chirpings are a brighter, higher-pitched version of those of the House Sparrow but more use is made of a hard rapid chittering. The nest is built by both sexes in a large hole in a tree or small hole in a building, wall, roof or cliff. Big colonies nest in the rows of drain-pipes in a reservoir embankment and some nest in old stone bridges. There are five or six eggs, smaller, darker and more variably blotched than House Sparrow eggs, and two or three broods. The Tree Sparrow is found across Europe and Asia to Japan and replaces the House Sparrow in China and Japan. It is frequently depicted in Japanese paintings.

HOUSE SPARROW
Passer domesticus

It is a mark of splendid rural isolation for a garden to be without a House Sparrow. This bird has attached itself to man and spread with him from Asia for the easy life gained from his crops, weeds and detritus. It is found only in cities, towns, villages and farmland and rarely uses anything other than a man-made structure for its nest. The number of House Sparrows must have decreased greatly since horse-drawn traffic disappeared from towns and combine harvesters appeared in the grain-fields so that neither street nor field is liberally spread with spilt grain. There are, however, still plenty of these birds and they will cling to the heads of oats to feed on the grain before the crop is cut. Flocks of several hundred birds gather at that time in fields and were thought to be city sparrows on a country holiday until they were shown to be the local families. The House Sparrow is seldom uninterested in mating and breeding. Mating is often intensive on a corner of guttering and nests may be being built at any time of year. The male does most of the building in any crevice on any structure and an untidy mass of straw and rubbish may project from a drainpipe, from fancy wrought iron work, a porch or lamp-post. Rarely a nest is built in a bush when it is neat and domed with a side entrance. This is one sign that the sparrow is not a finch but a weaver-bird. The four or five eggs are faintly green and heavily speckled. Three broods are raised. Noisy gatherings of several males and one female often take place, where the female soon departs and the males continue with their aggressive chirpings.

STARLING
Sturnus vulgaris

The Starling is the 'general purpose' bird. Unspecialised in any particular direction, it is very adaptable, a strong flier with a strong bill and a wide taste in food. Few natural or man-made features are not turned to advantage, from hatches of beetles on a mountain-top and ticks on cattle, to the sprinklers on sewage-farms – on the arms of which starlings seem to enjoy circular rides. From saltings and marshes to railway-sidings and dockyards, mown lawns or rubbish-tips, flocks of starlings are busy. Roosts of hundreds of thousands occur in young conifer plantations or on buildings in the centre of a city. For nesting, any cavity will suffice: a woodpecker-hole in a beechwood, or under a loose tile on a city house. The nest is an untidy gathering of straw and stems often extruding from the entrance, but has a cup lined with feathers, wool and moss inside. The male is often seen building the first part early in the year but the cup is added by the female after pairing. The five or six eggs are pale unspotted blue. A few seem to be left around, for one is often found undamaged on the lawn. The bird is usually silent in its level, rapid flight although the intention to fly is often announced by a crackling '*prrrrk*' and occasionally the panic call is given, a sharp '*plik*' which causes the birds to dive for cover when a Sparrowhawk is around. When perched or when feeding they use a medley of calls including a long descending whistle and a sharp rising one. Crowded on a bird-table, starlings brawl constantly with fierce chatterings, much lunging and some face-to-face hovering. The song is delivered at any time of year from an aerial, gutter or roof with more straining and effort than seems warranted by the result. Leaning forwards, with wings half flapped and throat bulging the starling splutters, whirrs and crackles but most birds mix with these some reasonably good mimicry. The Moorhen's '*carrook*' and the Pied Wagtail's '*chizzick*' are regular but some birds are more versatile.

JAY
Garrulus glandarius

Jays are small and colourful crows with much of the intelligence and cunning of the family. Our jay must use both these qualities in order to vanish as completely as it does when it is nesting, for it is a conspicuous bird at other times. Its harsh call is part of the scene in woodland and scrub everywhere except in the north of Scotland, and in recent years it has moved into the central Royal Parks in London. Persistent calls show the Jay to be keeping its wary eye on an intruder, whether a man or a cat, or to be mobbing its *bête noire*, the Tawny Owl. It has no true song but will sometimes show its vocal expertise by retiring to the centre of dense bushes and pouring forth a stream of mimicry together with a warbling chatter. Many calls and songs of other birds are accurately repeated and there may be neighing of horses or bleating of goats as well. Unlike the blue jays of America, our jay is pinkish-brown and black and white as normally seen; a departing bird seems to be mainly white rump and black tail. In sunlight the iridescent blue flashes on the inner wings may be seen from close quarters, and the blue feathers barred black from this patch are often found on the ground. The Jay feeds a great deal in spring on the eggs of small birds and some people dislike it for this reason – but they have no adverse effect on the numbers of their prey. Many clutches are replaced and in any case more small birds are reared each year than can be supported by the habitat. In autumn Jays pick acorns and fly with their crops bulging visibly, to enrich their territory by burying the acorns under long grass. When the acorns are finished the birds turn to sweet chestnuts.

MAGPIE
Pica pica

Magpies are moderate-sized crows with long tails and a glossy sheen on some of their plumage. In our bird the sheen is bright blue, showing green and orange from some angles, and is mainly on the tail. The name is a shortened form of 'Maggie-pie' or Black and white Maggie. This bird has spread greatly in the last thirty years, especially towards and sometimes into towns and cities. It is a noticeable feature of Dublin and has recently reached pest proportions in some city parks in Lancashire. One endearing quality of the Magpie is its abiding hatred of Carrion Crows: these coarse birds are harried relentlessly if they pass near a Magpie's nest, and cause highly vocal annoyance at any time. The Magpie tends to be noisy anyway, calling *'chack'* and *'chee-yok!'* or *'tchowk!'* a great deal, but the slightest annoyance causes a long hard chackering. It seldom flies far and the usual low short flights are dipping, but when it does go higher and further it flutters along fairly level with some shallow swoops and drops down steeply to land. It will visit bird-tables in small gardens briefly, sneaking in for the grosser scraps if it can before the starlings have mauled them. The nest is a domed 'fortress', often in a big thorn tree even by a busy road, built by both birds, and one clutch of about seven pale blue heavily speckled eggs is laid. In January up to a hundred or more Magpies may gather for a noisy ceremony of obscure function with much flying and chasing. On the ground the birds then move with big springy hops but at other times walking is more usual.

ROOK
Corvus frugilegus

This large black crow differs from the Carrion Crow in voice and habits as well as in its purple-glossed plumage, bare grey-white face and more tapered bill. The Rook is very much a bird of farmland and is only seen in woods or on commons if a plague of caterpillars of the Oak-Leaf Roller Moth attracts it there. Recently it has shown a great interest in the verges of motorways and in some parking-places on holiday routes. It used to be the traditional bird following the plough but now gulls have taken this over and the Rook does not care to mix much with those. It is the most social of all our land-birds and only accidentally is it sometimes without at least a dozen of its kind. A single pair cannot even breed successfully on its own but needs the clamour of a rookery. Within a rookery all is commotion, and thievery is rife. Despite legendary honesty and 'courts' for offenders, observation has shown that each stick is likely to pass through a dozen nests before coming to rest. Rookeries of a thousand nests were known a hundred years ago but there has been a decline in numbers of rooks, recently accelerated in some parts, and very few rookeries now have more than two hundred nests. They may be in any tall trees or the tallest available, which may be only six or seven metres, and can be on the ground if there are no trees. On winter evenings Rooks, often with Jackdaws, follow long-used flight-lines to their huge roosts, flying low against strong winds, high and playfully on fine days, when the constant call, '*carr*' is often high-pitched or yodelled.

CARRION CROW
Corvus corone

No bird in the countryside is harder to approach than is the Carrion Crow, but this is the big crow of city parks and town centres. It is this very wariness, coupled with a high intelligence that enable it to survive where few large birds can. In spring it will make dawn surveys of small gardens for nests to rob but it will be seen only when it makes a rapid swoop to seize a large fresh lump from the bird-table. Carrion Crows persistently perch high, often on the dead spikes at the tip of a Lombardy Poplar, and there they emit the coarsest calls. Leaning forward, fanning the tail for balance and bulging the throat with effort, they say '*aarraagh, aarraagh*' or perhaps '*kraerk!*' but sometimes it is the ridiculous 'motor-horn' note, a smooth high '*harnk-harnk*'. Normally seen only in pairs, these crows will in some areas, gather in the autumn evenings on fields or heaths to roost in hundreds. The nest is usually high in a solitary tree or small group of trees and is a large one of sticks, moss and earth, lined with wool, hair and feathers. About five eggs are laid and these may have a blue or green ground colour which may be unmarked or show any degree of brownish blotches, streaks or scrawls. The Carrion Crow is common north as far as Loch Lomond and Aberdeen but is replaced in the far north and in Ireland by the grey-bodied form, the Hooded Crow. This is mostly a bird of wilder places and seashores, seldom in cities and it has an even rougher voice, deeper and more raucous. The two forms hybridise in Central Scotland.

JACKDAW
Corvus monedula

This sociable little crow has not only some rather winning ways, it has blue eyes as well. It is usually associated with man, or rather with his buildings, and is relatively confiding for a crow. Whole colonies will fly around as a flock, but visibly as pairs within the flock and perch as a group of pairs. Jackdaws are talkative birds, seldom silent for long but chackering amongst themselves. The contact and flight note is a sharp '*chack*' and this could be the origin of the name Jackdaw as 'daw' is an old name for the Rook. However, 'jack' also is a word implying small and this is more probably the meaning. Jackdaws nest in belfries, ruins, cliffs, quarries and house chimneys, where their piling huge quantities of sticks can be a nuisance. They just drop sticks down until one lodges and the pile can be built to the required height. The nest is then lined with wool and hair and about five eggs are laid. These are pale bluish and may be almost unspotted, moderately, or densely marked with dark brown. The female alone sits and is fed on the nest by the male. Jackdaws with white bars in the wing or a white rump are occasionally seen. In flight, they have a more direct flight than the Rook and the noticeably smaller wings have a quicker action.

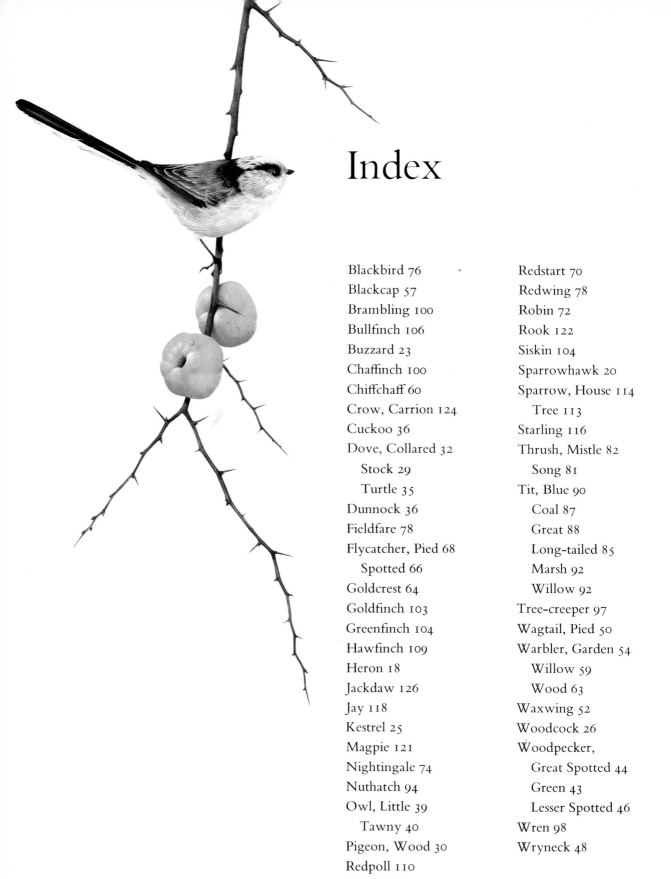

Index